Expressive Therapies
for Kids

Kimberley Palmiotto, PsyD, LCPC, ATR

Published by
PESI Publishing & Media
PESI, Inc.
3839 White Ave.
Eau Claire, WI 54703

Cover: Amy Rubenzer
Editing: Jenessa Jackson, PhD
Layout: Bookmasters, Amy Rubenzer
ISBN: 9781683732495

PESI
Publishing
& Media
pesipublishing.com

About the Author

Kimberley Palmiotto, PsyD, LCPC, ATR, is a licensed educational psychologist, registered art therapist, practicing clinical counselor, and school psychologist. Dr. Palmiotto has a Master's Degree in Marital and Family Therapy and a Doctorate in Educational Psychology as well as post-graduate training in school neuropsychology. She works with children, adolescents, families, and schools to help them understand the underlying learning and emotional needs that lead to a healthy and happy home and/or school culture.

Her personalized approach infuses research-based methods with the unique needs of clients to help them meet their goals in a fun, interactive way. She believes in a holistic approach by exploring with and educating clients about how mind, spirit, and body are interconnected.

Dr. Palmiotto has over 20 years of experience across a variety of treatment settings include; private practice, outpatient psychiatric, residential treatment centers for substance abuse, domestic violence shelters, public and private schools, and community based services.

Table of Contents

Chapter

1 Why Use the Expressive Arts in School Counseling?

2 Focus Areas Addressed with Expressive Therapies

3 Getting Started

4 Art and Drawing Directives

5 Music Directives

6 Play Directives

7 Drama Directives

Introduction

Working in the school system as a mental health professional has changed over the past decade. Currently, the profession requires much more from the school psychologist, school counselor, and school social worker than it has in the past. Previously, school mental health professionals have not been a primary focus of education. School counselors have often focused on academics, and school psychologists have often focused on testing and special education issues. As the student population has demonstrated more of a need in the area of mental health, these roles have expanded, and professionals in the field require more tools to deal with students' emerging needs. The school systems are in transition, and over the past few years, the necessity to address students' mental health needs has begun to make its way to the forefront. Cases such as Columbine, Newtown, and teen suicides related to bullying have given our society a collective pause to reflect on what we are doing to address the social-emotional and behavioral needs of our students.

The purpose of this book is to assist mental health professionals in reaching as many school-age children as possible by discussing how to weave in the expressive therapies within the context of school counseling. **Broadly speaking, the expressive therapies involve the use of the creative arts to help children communicate problems, process emotions, and develop solutions. The expressive therapies can include the therapeutic use of drama, visual arts, creative writing, play, dance/movement, and music—to name a few.**

Although most mental health professionals working within school systems have been trained in interventions related to the social-emotional and behavioral needs of students, fewer professionals have received information about how expressive therapies may be a useful addition to their "toolbox." For example, many school psychologists, counselors, and social workers use art and play in their daily activities with children, but they are unfamiliar with *how* these tools can be woven into the treatment plan to address their students' needs.

This book seeks to fill this gap by providing an introduction to the expressive therapies with the mental health professional in mind, as well as some specific directives and techniques that professionals can use when working with children in the school setting. Although there are a variety of forms of expressive therapies, this book will largely focus on the use of art, music, play, and drama therapy. These were chosen as methods that work well with children and adolescents, and are easily incorporated into counseling sessions both within the school setting as well as in a private practice setting.

For all the expressive therapies, there are specific educational considerations that should be mentioned for professionals considering pursuing accreditation. Art, music, and drama therapy have national organizations, which have developed specific criteria for accreditation. These organizations require professionals to have extended training and supervision in the areas of expertise to align themselves with other professionals in that specific area of expressive therapy. However, this does not preclude mental health professionals from using many of the expressive therapy techniques in their daily professional counseling duties. Indeed, many counselors often use expressive therapy techniques without the knowledge of why and how to use them proficiently. The purpose of this manual is to assist mental health professionals in understanding how and when to use the expressive therapies in a professional manner to best address the educational needs of the clients with which they are working.

Of note, the material in this book is not intended as a diagnostic tool for the expressive therapies but, rather, as a supplemental tool for your current practice. Certified, registered, or licensed expressive therapists have been through an extensive training and certification process. If you are interested in learning more about becoming a registered, certified, or licensed expressive therapist, you, can visit the following association websites to learn more about education, certification, and licensure requirements for any specific area of interest:

Art Therapy

- American Art Therapy Association: https://arttherapy.org
- Art Therapy Credentials Board: https://www.atcb.org

Music Therapy

- American Music Therapy Association: https://www.musictherapy.org

Drama Therapy

- North American Drama Therapy Association: http://www.nadta.org

Play Therapy

- Association for Play Therapy: https://www.a4pt.org

The concept of using expressive therapy techniques is not new, but integrating these therapies into school counseling can help you address the expanding needs of America's student body and bring out the best in the students you serve. By providing you with an understanding of how art, music, drama, and play can be incorporated into your work, it is my hope that this book will enhance your ability to develop the most appropriate plan for your clients and their families—and, more importantly, that these interventions will help you make a deeper impact on a larger number of students whom you serve.

Chapter 1

Why Use the Expressive Arts in School Counseling?

AN INTRODUCTION TO THE EXPRESSIVE ARTS

The expressive therapies involve the use of creative expression within the context of the therapeutic environment to help children process and communicate their thoughts and emotions. Some of the specific interventions involved include the use of dance/movement, drama, creative writing, poetry, art, play and sandtray. Although the expressive arts encompass a variety of different modalities and interventions, they are all associated with creative activities that children and adolescents usually enjoy. Different children may have different preferences, but, for the most part, children tend to find one or more of the arts an area that intrigues them and feels nonthreatening. Play is an integral part of how children learn; therefore, the introduction of counseling concepts through the natural form of art and play allows them to engage more easily and respond to topics that may be more challenging for them to do so in a more traditional talk therapy setting.

Although the expressive therapies are often thought of as "nonverbal" therapies, verbal communication is actually a key part of the process (Malchiodi, 2005). The nonverbal application paired with verbal discussion about the product itself makes the process less threatening, which allows children to lower their levels of defensiveness. The verbal discussion feels less about personal feelings and more about the product created or being created. The expressive activity itself becomes the catalyst for discussion and often is relied on throughout the process. Once engaged in the activity, whether it is art, music, play, or drama, verbal communication occurs as a part of the process, yet it is not the focus of the process. During the activity, the child is asked questions while performing the activity, as well as when reflecting on it afterward. This encourages them to use the process as a way to discuss their feelings, reflect on their own experiences or behaviors, or introduce coping strategies. Therefore, although there is a large component of nonverbal communication involved in the expressive therapies, it also relies on verbal communication in order to be truly effective.

This chapter provides an introduction to art, music, play, and drama therapies and highlights the benefit of including these interventions within the context of your practice with school-age children and adolescents.

Art

Art therapy is a creative intervention that focuses on the use of drawing, painting, sculpting, coloring, and other forms of art media to help students reflect on, process, and communicate their emotions. The tools themselves are not the important aspect in art therapy. Rather, the focus is on the process within the art that allows for more engagement and strategies for managing and discussing emotions and experiences. The efficacy of art therapy has been demonstrated across a variety of domains, including areas of social-emotional, behavioral, and academic development (Gonzalez-Dolginko, 2008). For example, research has found that art therapy is particularly useful in processing trauma, increasing self-esteem and self-expression, and addressing body image issues. It has also been found to increase attention span, decrease impulsivity, reduce acting-out behaviors, and increase self-awareness. Studies have also found that it may help students become more receptive to learning because it is associated with improved academic performance and a decrease in dropout rates (Gonzalez-Dolginko, 2008).

The therapeutic use of art is so effective for school-age children and adolescents because it bypasses their defense system and allows them to express their thoughts and feelings nonverbally. The artwork itself can include indicators of thoughts and feelings that the child is experiencing but is unable, or not yet ready, to communicate. For example, if you find consistent themes of death or violence in the artwork, then this might be an area to explore by discussing anxiety, anger, or depression and how to manage these emotions. As you begin to see themes in the expressive work done by a child, you can also utilize other modalities to encourage expression of a particular emotion or experience. Moving into storytelling or using drama techniques to act out scenes from the drawings may open a door to discussion about how the characters felt and managed their emotions. Whether or not the child is ready to discuss these thoughts and feelings is something to be decided from a treatment perspective, but it allows you to peek into the inner world of the student you are working with to better understand how to proceed with counseling in the future.

While the art that children create is not always straightforward or easy to understand, the wonderful thing about art therapy is that the end product is not the only benefit in the counseling process. Rather, the *process* of making the art is also a large component of the therapeutic process. Mandalas are one example of the process *and* product in art production. The process itself has research to support that the act of creating mandalas can reduce anxiety and increase mindful behaviors (DeLue, 1999). It lowers heart rate, slows breathing, and calms the centers of the brain that are related to anxiety. It encourages the child or adolescent to focus their attention and be present on one thing during the time they are working, which acts as a meditative, mindful moment. In addition, the product itself can be taken away as a token of the process or even used to reference later.

Music

Music therapy, which involves the therapeutic use of music to facilitate social and emotional well-being, is another beneficial intervention with children because it is inherently motivating, designed to focus on play, and is success-oriented such that children of all levels can succeed and feel a sense of mastery. It also encourages socialization and communication among participants. Music therapy is a "multimodal approach" in that it involves many of the senses, such as feeling and hearing through words/singing.

There are several reasons behind the utility of music as a therapeutic intervention. First, research has shown that human beings automatically respond to "feeling the beat." As humans, we inherently seek synchronization and respond on a primitive level to metronomic beats (Bergland, 2012). Think about the last time you heard your favorite song. Did you instinctively start tapping your feet or hands? Many times, this is the case, and we don't even realize it. Since rhythm is such an integral part of our human nature, it makes sense to involve music in counseling.

In addition, music is directly linked to our emotions. Research by Dr. Daniel Levitin—a former rock musician and now neuroscientist—has found that when humans sing together, oxytocin (a powerful hormone associated with emotional bonding) is released in the brain. His neuroimaging studies over the past 10 years have noted that music directly impacts brain structures that are involved in associative learning and emotional responses. Whether you are creating it or using it, music can be a powerful form of expression across childhood.

Similarly, neuroimaging research by Dr. Robert Zatorre has discovered that listening to pleasurable music engages the brain's reward system. In particular, music that people perceive as pleasurable causes the brain to release dopamine to the "feel good" center of the brain, which results in a sense of satisfaction and reward. What is important to consider is the subjectivity of what is considered pleasurable. Just as with art, music preferences are unique to each person. Not everyone finds "happy" songs to be pleasing or positive, and even songs traditionally labeled as "sad" may serve as a nostalgic reminder to some. Therefore, when using music as a therapeutic intervention, the key is to find music that appeals to the student you are working with, and not to you or others around them.

In addition, just as with any other stimuli that produce this "feel good" dopamine rush, music can be overused. Have you ever had a playlist that became predictable? Chances are, you have. Even your favorite songs can become annoying. One way to avoid this predictability is to shuffle playlists or use an online music program, such as Pandora®. In doing so, the anticipation of listening to a great song that strikes an emotional cord remains intact.

Play

Play therapy is a way for children to process through feelings that may be new or uncomfortable in a familiar context. It also allows for the introduction of coping strategies and tools for managing emotions in a way that is more easily accepted and internalized. Play is something that is intrinsic to each of us, and children use play not only as a way to interact with others but to communicate as well. Using play in a therapeutic model helps children learn and practice various ways to solve difficulties in a way that is familiar and fun.

Play therapy is an effective intervention for children because the language of play is a more natural form of communication for them (Cochran, 1996). It serves as a way for children to express their emotions or feelings in the same way that adults might utilize more traditional "talk therapy" (Axline, 1947). Play also allows children to reenact scenarios that they may not understand or have the cognitive ability to process through verbal discussion. Through the process of reenacting the scenario, including scenarios that they may have previously detached from, they often find a way to naturally process through their emotions.

One example of this phenomenon is the use of sandtray therapy. Through the use of a sand tray, a child can choose characters or other items that may possess the characteristics of the people or places involved in their life and use them to create stories or themes. In doing so, they are able to externalize their thoughts and feelings in a concrete manner without having to verbally explain the scenario as it happened. When children are given the opportunity to use this directive, they will often process through the issue on their own or be able to begin discussing the issue in relation to the themes in the sand tray, which can lead to more personal applications in their own life.

Drama

Drama therapy uses theatrical elements, such as stories, roles, scripted characters, and materials (e.g., puppets, costumes, masks, etc.)—and the enactment of these roles and stories—to help clients explore problems, gain insight, and eventually attain positive changes. Drama therapy can involve real or fantasy stories, and the child can either be involved in creating and telling the story or be a passive participant.

There are two commonly referenced approaches to drama therapy: psychoeducational drama and psychodrama (Urtz & Kahn, 1982). In psychoeducational drama, the drama directives are used to facilitate self-awareness about real-life problems. The child creates a "real-life" or familiar scene, reenacts it, and then relates it to their own lives. In psychoeducational drama, the presentation is time-limited (typically one to five minutes) and the real-life issue is left unresolved, often with the purpose of fostering further discussion about the issue (Urtz & Kahn, 1982). Psychodrama is similar in that the characters confront a real-life problem, but the process is usually longer, and the issue is always not left unresolved.

In addition, there are three main elements of drama therapy: play space, dramatic projection, and role-playing (Oon, 2010). *Play space* involves creating a space in which everything is play. Other than predetermined safety issues and rules, there are no consequences for actions, and children are given the freedom to experiment with different dramatic actions to encourage spontaneity. *Dramatic projection* allows children to project their underlying feelings on to a character or role that they are playing. As children project their inner experience via theatrical enactments or dramatic materials, they are able to externalize their inner conflict. This, in turn, allows mental health professionals to identify the conflict and develop a plan for addressing it using similar, nonthreatening interventions. The last component of drama therapy, *role-playing*, allows children to explore and create new ideas of themselves. They are exposed to different roles—and witness and reflect on others as their peers fill various roles as well—which allows them to gradually modify their self-perceptions.

Using drama with school-age children has a unique way of tapping into their creativity and humor while indirectly teaching them a variety of skills. In particular, drama therapy can help them gain social skills, find different ways to connect with peers, improve their ability to regulate their emotions, and understand how empathy works in relation to others. It achieves this through the use of sensory experiences to explore items or environments, as well as improvisation. Once a child or adolescent is comfortable with these techniques, they can move to role-play, which can be more personalized to their experiences.

THE CASE FOR EXPRESSIVE THERAPIES IN SCHOOL-BASED COUNSELING

Although school-based counseling has been part of the public school structure for many years, it has changed in form and delivery as the public school system has evolved. In the 1990s, the public schools moved from solely providing academic support toward the inclusion of health and mental health services as well. In turn, specific educational staff were added to provide these services to students (Schlechty, 1990). Initially, public schools began providing a multitude of services as part of this movement, but doing so put a financial strain on the public school system, and many of these services were eventually cut in various districts that could not afford to keep them in place. This prompted the drafting of laws, such as the Individuals with Disabilities Education Act, to address these disparities. While these laws were certainly well-intentioned, their focus was exclusively on the provision of services within the context of special education, which left students in the general education population without support.

As mental health professionals, when we talk about helping our clients, the conversation often becomes more about academics than issues related to mental health. However, as academic demands have increased over the years, we have underestimated the impact that these demands have on our children. For example, a recent study noted that in children aged three to seventeen years, 7.1% had current anxiety problems, 7.4% had a current behavioral/conduct problem, and 3.2% had current depression (Ghandour et al., 2019). Additionally, the U.S. Census Bureau conducted the 2016 National Survey of Children's Health (NSCH) survey of parents in the United States, which resulted in 17.4% of children aged two to eight years documented to have at least one mental, behavioral, and/or developmental disorder (CDC, 2018).

Therefore, it is imperative to include mental health support programs in our schools. This need has gradually been recognized by the educational community, as evidenced by increased funding and programs for educationally related mental health services. Although many new programs are being developed, many still rely solely on traditional methods, which can seem somewhat threatening or even cliché to some children and adolescents. Children who have experienced forms of traditional "talk therapy" often come into counseling with certain expectations that they will be asked about their feelings, which can be overwhelming if they do not have the language to describe them. In addition, asking children to focus on feelings and problem solve a situation may too closely parallel the directives from school-wide or classroom management interventions. This can turn the sessions into extensions of the classroom and not a place that spurs creativity and expression.

To engage students in the counseling process, we need to make it appealing and nonthreatening to them. Utilizing the expressive therapies is one way to attain this goal while reducing anxiety and pressure on students. **The arts are a natural tool toward which children and adolescents gravitate, and it provides a nonthreatening medium through which they can communicate underlying thoughts and feelings that they may otherwise be unable to express.** Given this, expressive therapies are a wonderful tool that can assist the mental health professional in addressing the social, emotional, and/or behavioral needs of students who may otherwise be difficult to reach.

Although there are many public school districts across the nation that utilize school-based counseling, there are very few that formally integrate expressive therapies into their programs. However, one program that has managed to integrate the expressive therapies into its services is the Miami-Dade County Public Schools' Art Therapy Department (Isis, Bush, Siegel, & Ventura, 2010). Currently, the program employs 16 clinical art therapists that service students from kindergarten through 12th grade. Launched as a one-year pilot program in 1979, this program has continued to grow and has evolved into an integral part of the special education program in this county. Although the program started as a service to all students with a variety of special needs, its current focus is on improving the emotional functioning of students with emotional and behavioral difficulties (Bush, 1997). They continue to be at the forefront of the integration of the arts in mental health in schools. The program has provided research to support the effectiveness of programs like this across the country, as well as support and models for how to guide other mental health professionals in finding ways to include art therapy as an inclusive model in schools with special education.

Focus Areas Addressed with Expressive Therapies

EDUCATIONALLY RELATED MENTAL HEALTH SERVICES

If you are a mental health professional working with a child in the school system, then you know that the goals developed within the context of the child's treatment plan must be "educationally related." There is a fine and blurry line drawn when it comes to mental health services in the school system, and guidelines stipulate that we are only allowed to work on mental health issues that are educationally related in nature. Although it is possible to define what constitutes an educationally related goal (e.g., it involves any issue that is directly impacting a child's educational performance), I always have to laugh a little at the attempt to fit mental health in this box because, realistically, *all mental health issues impact education in one form or another.*

That being said, I have spent years in the public school system and absolutely understand the need to differentiate between these types of goals. As mental health professionals, we encounter a variety of disabilities and mental health issues in the school system so it is important that we do not become responsible for larger issues that are not directly related to school. If an issue is identified as being educationally related in nature, then it qualifies for educationally related mental health services (ERMHS), which fall under the provision of special education services and are documented through an Individualized Education Program (IEP). There are emerging programs for both general education and special education students to address educationally related mental health needs. For the most part, general education counseling tends to focus on issues such as bullying, social skills, and anxiety. It is focused on skill building without these challenges directly having a negative impact on overall educational performance.

In contrast, when a child receives an IEP with educationally related mental health issues to be addressed, then the goals in counseling tend to be more focused on helping remediate or build skills deficits in the area of mental health. For example, it may be that a child has difficulties managing anxiety but is easily redirected and tends to require minimal support in managing these challenges within the classroom without it impacting their educational performance. However, if these issues become more severe and they demonstrate an adverse impact on educational performance, then this child might meet the criteria for special education services, which could ultimately help them develop and use coping strategies to manage these behaviors. It is a more direct intervention focused on an identified deficit that is specific to a student.

Although what constitutes a qualifying diagnosis for an IEP falls along the same lines as traditional mental health diagnoses, the special education categories can also be broader and more general in nature. For example, some of the most common qualifying disabilities that I have encountered include: autism spectrum disorder (or autism-like characteristics), attention-deficit/hyperactivity disorder (ADHD), emotional disturbance, and other health impairment (which is an umbrella term to describe deficits in strength or alertness that impact a student's ability to attend to the educational environment). Within these categories, there also tends to be overlapping issues to be addressed.

As you may have gathered from some of the broader terms such as "emotional disturbance" and "other health impairment," not all qualifying conditions are exclusive to mental health needs. Obviously, any child that is found to have a unique social, emotional, or behavioral need may qualify for ERMHS. For example, I have worked with individuals whose "other health impairment" included diagnoses such as cerebral palsy, Tourette's syndrome, traumatic brain injury, and even learning disabilities. The criteria itself doesn't matter; the core issue is that their condition is impacting their educational performance.

In the section that follows, I'll discuss a few of the disorders, symptoms, and disabilities that may be included in these special education categories and how expressive therapies may be of benefit. In addition, I will describe how children's unique social-emotional, behavioral, and academic needs can be addressed through various expressive therapy interventions. Finally, I will discuss the importance of considering a child's age when implementing expressive therapies, as elementary versus secondary school-age children have unique and important qualities to consider.

MATCHING TECHNIQUE TO DIAGNOSIS

Autism Spectrum Disorder

Expressive therapists have worked with children on the autism spectrum in a variety of ways, both in educational settings and in private practice. Although all forms of expressive therapies can be beneficial when working with children on the spectrum, art therapy is particularly useful because it helps address their primary deficits in communication and spontaneous imagination. In particular, "the creative act necessary in the making of art is itself an act of imagination. It involves the translation of an internal image in the mind into a tangible form on the sheet of paper" (Evans & Dubowski, 2001, p. 8). In other words, creating a painting or making a drawing is an act of communication because when we create an image, we expect that others will be able to understand what it is and what we are trying to communicate in some way.

In early intervention, art therapy can be utilized to increase a child's basic engagement with others as well as build their motor skills and visual spatial skills. These skills can also be utilized with older children who have a diagnosis of autism spectrum disorder (ASD), although there are other areas that can also be addressed with the use of art, such as social communication, sensory processing, and increasing verbal communication of feelings and needs. The basic act of engaging in the expressive therapies can often provide an opportunity for social communication with peers and adults. Between the interactions for directions and review of the product/process, there are multiple opportunities for verbal communication, as well as teaching opportunities for understanding nonverbal social cues in sessions.

Drama therapy is another form of expressive therapy that has been studied and utilized effectively with children diagnosed with ASD. In particular, drama therapy has been found to improve social communication, reduce anxiety, and increase cognitive flexibility among children with ASD (Godfrey & Haythorne, 2013). It also helps children better understand the perspectives of others and improves their ability to recognize other people's faces. One reason behind the efficacy of drama therapy is that the introduction and use of role-playing, movement, and body language helps foster an understanding of how to communicate with (and interpret communication from) others. Engaging in a drama directive requires that children assess and gather social information in order to participate in the activity. They must focus on social cues to react and respond in certain situations. Additionally, they must practice cognitive flexibility when asked to participate in improvisation activities, where they have to think quickly and change their response or perspective based on the information and feedback they are being given.

When working with students on the autism spectrum, be sure to spend as much time as needed building rapport and making them feel comfortable in the environment. Depending on the child's level of functioning, you may be able to use a variety of directives that can build on their current educational goals by encouraging and modeling social skills, skills building, social language, life skills, and even concepts related to abstract or higher-level thinking. A thorough pre-assessment is imperative to understand the specific strengths and challenges associated with the student's learning profile. This assessment can include observations, historical data, and even doing a bit of your own informal assessment (as needed and appropriate) on the student's cognitive functioning, social skills, social language abilities, and sensory needs.

Understanding a student's specific sensory needs is especially important so you don't inadvertently introduce materials or an environment that produces anxiety or frustration. Therefore, sensory processing is an area that should be reviewed continuously when using art or other modalities that might include the senses. For example, when working with music, keeping the music to no more than 60 beats per minute is typically best to avoid sensory overload. Knowing what specific aversions a student has, or whether there are any restrictions on materials they can have access to, will help avoid many possible roadblocks to effective intervention. This, in turn provides you with more opportunities to involve them in novel experiences, including those that involve social engagement.

In addition, understanding how other professionals work effectively with the student will be helpful in building rapport (Evans & Dubowski, 2001). Don't be afraid to ask other providers and specialists who work with your client for their suggestions and feedback on what they have found to work best. You might find that many of these same accommodations and approaches benefit your time with the student as well.

Anxiety

Although anxiety is not an eligibility criterion for ERMHS in the school system, it is an underlying current in the emotional realm of many students regardless of their qualifying disability. Therefore, I find that it is an important category to discuss since anxiety can be pervasive across conditions. Some of the most common anxiety-based disorders that impact students include separation anxiety, generalized anxiety, school phobia, and obsessive-compulsive disorder. Additionally, comorbidity with other diagnoses is very common, especially ADHD and ASD.

In my own professional experience as a school psychologist, I have seen the rates of anxiety (whether formally diagnosed or not) rise dramatically among children and adolescents over the last 20 years. Although there is an ongoing debate for the reason behind this upsurge, the reality is that increasing numbers of students (both in the general and special education population) are presenting to my practice with symptoms of anxiety that are significant enough to represent a functional disturbance. Given this, I always find that it is helpful to thoroughly assess for symptoms of anxiety during an initial intake with a child. Sometimes, anxiety can be the underlying cause of some of the other externalizing (or even internalizing) behaviors we see with referrals, such as school refusal, selective mutism, and somatic complaints.

For example, school refusal and somatic complaints are symptoms that are commonly associated with several anxiety disorders. Often, children will be referred due to problems with consistently leaving class or excessive health office referrals with no documented health issues. Many times, educational staff may dismiss this behavior as defiance or "overreacting" because they misunderstand the underlying anxiety related to the behavior. Identifying what is causing the anxiety is imperative, as doing so will allow you to get to the root of what is prompting students to leave class or develop somatic symptoms.

Some of the best expressive therapy interventions for anxiety involve mindfulness and helping clients develop self-awareness surrounding their current state of mind so that they can evaluate and make appropriate changes in their thinking. Using cognitive-behavioral strategies in conjunction with art, music, and play can be especially beneficial for students presenting with anxiety because it allows children to move past the words and language that might limit their ability to process the strategies.

Mandala art therapy is another technique that has been found to be effective in reducing anxiety in children. Using mandalas involves creating a geometric design, often in the form of a circle, and filling it in with different patterns and symbols. One reason that mandalas are effective in reducing anxiety is because the design process of creating the mandala is centering and helps restore a sense of balance. Indeed, research conducted with school-age children has found that creating mandalas results in subsequent physiological changes that represent a relaxation response, such as decreased heart rate and autonomic arousal (DeLue, 1999). In addition, creating mandalas is a simple enough task that children can work on while in the health office or even during a "break" outside of class. Once they feel calmer, they may be able to reenter the classroom or at least have a discussion with a trusted staff member about developing a plan to return.

Selective Mutism

Selective mutism is a rare but complex disorder. It involves an extreme form of social anxiety in which children will not speak in specific social situations, often out of fear of embarrassment. It impacts both social and academic functioning and often causes students to be isolated. It usually becomes evident once students enter a school setting, and although they may be completely mute at school, they present as a normal developing child at home or in alternate environments of comfort (Phelps, 2006). Expressive therapies are especially useful with children who present with selective mutism due to their nonverbal nature. Using expressive therapies gives students an opportunity to convey their feelings without feeling the pressure to talk.

Although there is little research with drama therapy and selective mutism, the results of a particular case study with a five-year-old girl show promise. In particular, using drama therapy in combination with behavioral shaping helped the girl develop spontaneity of speech and also shaped the emergence of an extraverted and playful personality (Oon, 2010). One reason that drama therapy may be effective with selective mutism is that the process of role-playing in the context of the drama directive naturally invites speech, as the child must usually speak to take on a role. It allows children to participate and be a part of a social interaction with others without forcing them to speak or increasing their anxiety. The child has a choice in how much or how little to participate in both the action and the discussion in their role. Additionally, they may also choose to take on the role of the director, which allows the mental health professional an opportunity to observe their thought process as they direct scenes and create roles of people involved. Drama also allows for nonverbal role-playing and interaction such as pantomime. Given that the process of role-playing can help naturally elicit spontaneous speech, a game like charades is another great way to encourage this interaction.

ADHD

Often, children with ADHD have difficulty applying what they have learned due to problems with impulsivity, distractibility, and inattention. These issues cause them to either miss, misinterpret, or omit information that they may have previously been taught or mastered. It is for this reason that art therapy can be a particularly effective tool for ADHD: When a child creates a piece of art, it becomes a tangible memory that they can refer to throughout the course of treatment. Specifically, it provides a concrete benchmark at the initial intake session and serves as a visual representation of their progress throughout the remainder of treatment (Safran, 2002).

In addition to art therapy, music and play therapy are also valuable tools when working with children who struggle with inattention and impulsivity. Both of these modalities provide children an opportunity to build some self-awareness around their current set of skills, as well as to build some skills along the way. For example, "Red Light/Green Light" (page 107) is a game that can help children develop better impulse control and attentional skills, as they must learn to listen carefully to the leader's commands and utilize self-control to stop when "red light" is called. Music can be used in a similar way to introduce and practice techniques to manage impulsivity and distractibility. Musical activities that provide opportunities to stop and start and self-monitor, such as call and response singing or drum circles, are great tools to use.

Mindfulness is another great tool to include in treatment plans for children and adolescents with ADHD. Starting this journey can be overwhelming for these students because asking them to sit still and be present in the here-and-now is almost painful. They would probably rather be doing *anything* else! However, in my experience, as students begin to master the skill of mindfulness, they start to understand its benefit in reducing their racing thoughts, calming their mind, and increasing their focus.

The tricky part about introducing mindfulness to children with ADHD is determining where to start. You don't want to overwhelm your client by introducing a skill that is too difficult in the beginning. I have found that starting with guided visualization is a great place to begin, as it does not have the word "meditation" in it, which often can trigger defensiveness in some clients. As you build rapport and help children develop trust with this intervention, they may be more willing to try the next steps, which might include a more mindful meditative approach (see Chapter 4).

In my practice, one tool that has been extremely beneficial as a transitional tool between guided visualization and independent meditation is the MUSE headset and app, which can be found on Amazon or at https://choosemuse.com. The app teaches mediation by providing concrete audio feedback about brain activity while the client meditates. If clients are in a state of relaxation, then they hear gentle nature sounds, such as the soothing sound of an ocean or forest. However, if they become distracted, then the headband uses neurofeedback to sense this, and it provides escalating environmental sounds until they are able to refocus.

Emotional Disturbance

Students with emotional or behavioral disturbances often present with a host of issues, including depression, low self-esteem, anxiety, aggression, anhedonia, impulsivity, and resistance to authority. In general, most students who have a qualifying condition of an emotional disturbance have participated in some form of therapeutic intervention in the past, with talk therapy being the primary modality. However, the expressive therapies are of particular benefit with these students because their directives bypass the traditional therapeutic approaches that the students have been exposed to in the past (Isis et al., 2010; McIntyre, 2007; Sausser & Waller, 2006).

Compared to traditional approaches, the expressive therapies generally involve a less intrusive interaction and allow students more control over the topics of conversation. For example, instead of asking children to talk about or verbally solve problems on their own, they are creating and developing art, which is a much less threatening form of communication. These factors often open a window that has been closed tightly in the past, allowing the counselor to build rapport and ultimately make progress toward each student's goals.

When working with students with emotional or behavioral disturbances, it is often easier to engage students who are primarily dealing with anxiety and depression, as they tend to be more open to interventions. In contrast, students who have a history of defiance and aggression can demonstrate more resistance and will often require additional time to build rapport and engage them in the process. These students often crave (and even demand) control, so providing them with as many choices as possible can help in rapport building. Providing them with choices can happen in a number of ways, from letting them choose the particular activity at hand to letting them lead groups or create activities. Often, starting with topics that are of interest to them and creating activities around that helps increase engagement.

Intellectual Disability

In the expressive therapies, the goals for students with intellectual disabilities are different than those for other populations. The focus is much more on the process and product itself, versus trying to make any interpretations about the student's creation. Many students with intellectual disabilities have difficulty understanding directions, which can lead to a completely different end product than originally intended. However, it is not the finished product that is of therapeutic value to students with intellectual disabilities.

Rather, it is the joy that comes from *creating* something and the sense of pride that comes from *sharing* that with the people involved in the process (West, 2012). Therefore, processing and interpreting are not areas of focus when related to the finished product. Instead of asking reflective questions at the end of the session, the focus is more about the process of making the expressive piece.

There are many opportunities in session to introduce and reinforce skill building with students who have intellectual disabilities, and the use of expressive therapies is a great tool to accomplish this goal. For example, songs can be used to teach children skills in a fun and creative atmosphere. In addition, if the song is something that the student can learn and memorize, then you can utilize it as a tool to support and reinforce skills. The song becomes something that is predictable and familiar; in turn, clients often respond positively when it is sung to them or when they are asked to sing it in specific circumstances as a teachable moment. A perfect example of this is the "Clean Up" song that is often used with younger children. The song is first introduced to children while they are cleaning up so that when the song is played later, it serves as a cue for them to clean up their areas and move on to another activity.

Additionally, many expressive therapy activities can help students with intellectual disabilities learn social skills or life skills in a fun and engaging way. One way to accomplish this is to use your sessions to create tools that students can use outside of your time together. For example, you can create "Power Cards" for clients that incorporate their favorite superhero, or even pictures of clients engaging in specific behaviors that are included in their educational or life skills goal bank (e.g., raising their hand in class or listening when the teacher is talking). One side of the card contains the picture of the superhero or student, and the other side contains the specific goal in writing. These cards can be used in class or at home to remind students about certain behaviors and goals they are working on at specific times during the day.

Another important consideration when working with intellectual disabilities is collaboration with other providers. If you have the opportunity to collaborate with other providers working with the student (e.g., speech and language therapist, special education teacher, occupational therapist), then this can open new doors for creativity. These providers can give you ideas about goals and skills that you may not see in your sessions, which can allow you to create some unique and individualized tools for the student. You might be surprised at how many things you come up with when you have more than one view of the client. It may be as simple as working with the speech therapist to create some songs about social skills that can be used in both sessions. Or, perhaps you find that the occupational therapist is working on handwriting, so you create a game that includes writing letters or words, or tracing items. Thinking outside the box is key in these situations. The more creative, the better.

OTHER AREAS OF FOCUS

In addition to addressing specific qualifying diagnoses within the special education sector, the expressive therapies are an effective tool that can address children's unique social-emotional, behavioral, and academic needs. In particular, research has found that the expressive therapies help children process traumatic events, promote the development of social skills, improve impulse control and emotion regulation skills, and facilitate academic growth (Gonzales-Dolginko, 2008). In this section, I'll touch on each of these topics in further detail and discuss how the expressive therapies can be of benefit.

Social-Emotional Development

When working with a child who is processing through a traumatic event, it is very possible that you may be the secondary professional working with that child as they transition back to school. Therefore, as a school counselor, an important part of your role is to help that student develop a plan to manage their symptoms as they arise in the school setting. In addition, using expressive therapies can often help bridge the gap between the skills the student is learning and mastering with the primary provider, which can aid in the transition back into the school environment.

When we talk about trauma, it is important to note that trauma does not have to include a single isolated incident. For example, if you are working in a low socioeconomic area, you should be cognizant of the fact that many of the children you work with live in a constant state of stress. They may worry about having their daily needs met; witness domestic violence; be exposed to drugs, alcohol, and other illicit paraphernalia; or live in a violent neighborhood. Essentially, they live in a state of perpetual trauma that they must cope with on a daily basis. It is important to keep all of these factors in mind because, often, a lack of progress in treatment may simply reflect a lack of basic needs as opposed to challenges with higher-level processing. In these situations, you must work to tailor your interventions both educationally and therapeutically to meet the needs of these students.

Another "typical trauma" that many children and adolescents experience these days is divorce. We don't often think of divorce as a trauma, but for children who are experiencing it, divorce definitely is traumatic! Let's face it, the majority of divorces are not amicable, and parents struggle with how to manage their own emotions while still taking into account their children's feelings. The stress that children experience in the context of a divorce can result in anxiety, depression, and other problems that can benefit from the use of expressive therapies. For example, children can create trauma timelines within the context of art therapy to provide a visual narrative of their trauma story. Music therapy is another modality that can help children express their feelings by tapping into emotional experiences linked to the music or providing them with opportunities to change the script in their head with lyrics or music. Drama therapy can also be effective in allowing children to act out specific challenges and reframe the narrative surrounding their trauma.

In addition to trauma, other areas of social-emotional development that are likely to emerge when counseling school-age children include problems with social communication, friendships, anxiety, depression, relational aggression, and bullying. Using the expressive therapies with these topics can serve as a wonderful entry point to further discussion and pave the way for the use of more specific and evidence-based interventions, such as cognitive-behavioral therapy and brief solution-focused therapy. For example, the art therapy directive of "What Is Your Superpower?" (page 40) can help you identify what children perceive as their strengths (aka "superpowers") and weaknesses. This, in turn, can lead to further discussion surrounding how children can use these "superpowers" outside of session to strengthen any perceived weaknesses.

The expressive therapies can also facilitate children's social-emotional development on a more global level through the use of larger-scale group projects. For example, if allowed, you can ask students to use their phones, or you can provide them with cameras, to take pictures around the school that describe the school culture and environment. These pictures can then be brought back to the group and discussed. This type of larger project can help create positive school-wide campaigns about topics like kindness or bullying, or help define and change school climate when used with administration or other educational staff.

Behavioral Issues

As previously discussed within the context of ADHD, the expressive therapies can help children increase attention span, decrease impulsivity, and reduce acting-out behaviors. However, even for children who do not have a formal diagnosis of ADHD, executive functioning challenges are one area that seem to generate the most referrals for mental health professionals. In my experience, this is because after a certain amount of time, children with executive functioning difficulties become anxious, depressed, and present with a sense of inadequacy. We all want to succeed, and children who have these difficulties often don't get to feel the same successes as other kids. They are constantly being told to "refocus, listen, calm down, and stop doing that."

Most children with executive function difficulties will not enter your doors until about third or fourth grade. For their first few years in school, they may manage to keep hope alive and try over and over again, but unless they achieve some form of success within that time frame, they begin to lose their sense of confidence and anxiety builds. Once they hit this point, these students will either become the "class clown" or start acting out behaviorally. Once these behavioral difficulties have emerged, the expressive therapies may not be the magic bullet, but they may be a window into their thought patterns and feelings that would not otherwise be available.

For example, in contrast to traditional talk therapy, the expressive therapies can help children uncover aspects of themselves that they were not otherwise aware of since these tools often bypass the "intellectual thinking" part of the brain. For example, in the "Bridge Drawing" intervention (page 48), students are asked to draw a bridge from one place to another, with an arrow representing directionality and a dot representing where they are on the bridge. When students initially draw the line, they do so from a place of abstract thought. However, when you ask them to place themselves on the bridge, it becomes a more personal representation of their life journey. As you begin to discuss the past and future in their drawing, and where they are in this process, you start to see the connections happen. These types of insightful discussions can still happen in traditional talk therapy, but the use of expressive therapies can decrease guarded responses and resistance. It is for this reason that you will often see "aha" moments with your clients in session, especially when working with older students who have the capability to engage in higher-level thinking strategies.

In addition, the expressive therapies can help address any anger, disrespect, or aggressive behaviors that children may exhibit as a result of their frustration or feelings of helplessness. Children who are prone to behavioral outbursts can especially benefit from learning and mastering emotion-regulation skills, which can be woven into many of the expressive therapy interventions. One particular example is crinkle art therapy, in which children create a piece of art out of an angry episode. Specifically, when children are angry or beginning to escalate, you ask them to crinkle up a piece of paper as hard and tight as they want to. Once they have sufficiently crinkled it up, you ask them if they want to see how this crinkled ball can turn into something beautiful. Once they answer yes (it may take time), unfold the paper and lay it on a flat surface. Point out that there are some different shapes that the crinkles have made on the paper, and ask the child to use some colored pencils or markers to see if they can color in the shapes and create a design with the crinkled folds. Given that the act of coloring is calming and centering, by the end of the session you might see a change in the child's demeanor—*and* they have a wonderful art piece to take with them. This type of intervention can help children learn how they can turn something challenging into something positive.

Academic Skills

Not only can the expressive therapies address social-emotional and behavioral needs, but they can lead to improvements in academic performance and decreases in dropout rates as well (Gonzalez-Dolginko, 2008). Although there do not seem to be any specific academic skills that are remediated by the expressive therapies, the general idea is that if students are emotionally stable and happy, then they can better focus on their studies and graduate. Indeed, a study in 2015 found that the use of expressive therapies in schools led to an overall increase in the feeling of "well-being" among students (Barnes-Smith, Frotz, Ito, Kohorst, & Vascimini). When students are in a positive state of mind, any emotional barriers to learning are removed, which opens the door for learning and accepting feedback.

Often, students are referred to counseling for issues that may be secondary to, or directly related to, an underlying academic challenge. For example, many clients I see have specific goals related to anxiety or depressive symptoms. However, as we begin our sessions and I learn more about them, these issues often stem from how they view themselves and their ability to learn. These students have had repeated challenges with learning that have led to feelings of helplessness and frustration, and after experiencing this frustration for years, feelings of anxiety, depression, and low self-esteem begin to emerge. In these cases, it is obviously important to address the emotional issues at hand, but it is also important to simultaneously work with educational staff to make sure that the student's educational goals address the underlying issues related to learning and academics. For example, a goal may be developed to help a student utilize appropriate coping strategies when emotionally escalated so that student can perform efficiently in the classroom. This collaboration can occur with the student's special education and general education teacher, as well as any other specialists working with the client.

AGE AND THE EXPRESSIVE THERAPIES

If you are a mental health professional and have worked with K–12 clients, then you know that elementary and secondary-aged children are very different. With regard to the expressive therapies, it is important to remember that at the elementary level, it is all about fun and self-expression. In early elementary school, there is usually minimal resistance and children can easily engage in a variety of activities and techniques without a lot of prompting or encouragement. As students move into the upper elementary grades, you might begin to see a slight decline in the "fun factor" as children become more conscientious of their product. For example, in early elementary school, children tend to get very excited about the idea of playing a role-playing game, but as children move into the upper elementary school years, this idea may begin to cause them some anxiety because of their experiences with being "embarrassed about performing," which may or may not have caused some previous embarrassment.

When this occurs, it can be helpful for you, as the counselor, to join in on any directives that require the production of some end product. For example, if performing a role-play, you can join in as a character to help guide a theme or topic. In general, directives and activities that are more play-oriented tend to produce less anxiety. However, with all activities, if you join in and demonstrate that students will not be judged, then it is much easier to build rapport, and children tend to engage in each of the processes more fluidly. (See Chapter 4 for more information about joining in.)

As students enter secondary level education, they may initially be more defensive to engage in the therapeutic process, but as they become more comfortable and develop stronger rapport with you, this defensiveness should decrease and be replaced by feelings of acceptance. The expressive therapies help to make students at this age feel more supported and less judged than traditional "talk therapy" alone. In addition, group work and techniques like drama therapy tend to be peer-oriented, which is a developmental focus for students at this age.

Chapter

Getting Started

WHEN IS THE BEST TIME TO USE THE ARTS IN SCHOOL-BASED COUNSELING?

The short answer to this question is: Anytime! The arts are an area that children naturally gravitate toward regardless of their socioeconomic status, age, family history, or gender. Most children enjoy some form of music, fantasy play, or visual arts, whether it be singing, creating music, dramatic play, drawing, painting, mask-making, papier-mâché, crafts, watercolor, or clay. There is usually some form of art that intrigues a child. A child who does not enjoy drawing may love manipulating clay or creating ceramics, just as a child who is indifferent toward the visual arts may actively seek out and have a passion for music.

The great thing about using the arts in school-based counseling is that you can integrate it at any point during the counseling sessions. However, if you have a client who is very shy and is having difficulty sharing verbally, then it may be best to introduce art in the beginning sessions to help with establishing rapport and building trust in the relationship. Vice versa, if a child is hyperverbal in sessions, then it may be helpful to introduce art throughout the course of the session to help redirect the discussion or encourage self-reflection. When you are deciding when and how to incorporate art, remember that *no matter when it is done, it can be beneficial in some way.*

Preference Menu: Deciding on a Medium

When deciding which modality to use, it is important to understand the student's level of comfort with the different mediums you have available. This is best accomplished by producing a sort of menu of mediums at the beginning of treatment that the child can "try out." Picking and choosing items can actually become a very fun activity because most students have not been exposed to all types of mediums, so there is usually at least one new thing they will encounter.

Introducing these various mediums does not have to be done over an inordinate amount of sessions. In fact, you could provide a sampling of each medium in one session by presenting them in a menu format on a large table and providing plenty of room for the student to experiment with each one. Start by briefly explaining each of the items on the table, and then present them one by one to the student, allowing approximately five minutes for each medium. After each sample, ask the client to rate the likability of that medium using a Likert scale of 1 to 5. These ratings will serve as your master copy that will assist you in developing future treatment plans using various art mediums.

It's also important to discuss students' experiences after each sampling to better understand the reasons behind their ratings. Don't just ask students how they liked the item or how it made them feel, but ask more specific questions, such as:

- *Did using that make you feel more calm or anxious?*
- *What was your favorite part about that activity?*
- *What was the thing you liked least about that activity?*

After you have cycled through each of the mediums, give students the option to choose which one they would like to use the next time you use art in your session. Doing so will help you develop a specific treatment plan surrounding that medium, and students will more than likely be excited about using art in upcoming sessions. It can also provide a level of anticipation that usually leads to the student asking, "So when can we do that again?"

In general, you will be able to tell immediately whether or not a student is engaged in the art process. If they are not, it may be related to their dislike of the medium itself, which can result from a variety of factors, such as lack of exposure to the medium or a sensory issue surrounding it. It is important to not become polarized in your response if this occurs. Don't jump to "dumping" the medium forever, and definitely don't force it on the student during sessions. Simply move it to the back of the line, keeping it accessible for future use if needed. It may be that as the student moves through other issues, they become more open to experimenting with that medium in the future.

SOME ISSUES THAT MAY COME UP

Regardless of your planning, perfect scheduling, research, and general optimism, *you will encounter roadblocks.* Just like with any other form of counseling, your clients will present with certain issues that may either interrupt progress or stop it from starting in the first place. By allowing yourself the freedom to accept and embrace this fact, you will move through these issues much easier.

Resistance

Resistance is not uncommon in expressive therapy groups with students who are new to the modalities, especially older clients and family members. They tend to see many of these things as "younger" tools. Therefore, it is helpful to approach the client's resistance by attempting to understand the root of the resistance.

When students refuse or resist participating in sessions, you must first ask yourself if you are using the appropriate materials or type of expressive therapy appropriate for them. A pre-assessment, which is completed prior to initiating sessions, should help determine where to begin. The pre-assessment should include a review of records along with a basic interview to determine the student's preference for art materials and alternate expressive modalities. For example, do they love music but hate drawing? Is there an observed trend of increased attendance in their elective drama class? When you interview them, do you come to find out they have refused to draw or paint since elementary school because they were a victim of teasing and became self-conscious?

These factors, in addition to the preference menu discussed earlier, are all things that you should try to uncover prior to developing a treatment plan for the student.

Of course, not all of this information is needed at the very start, and you should be prepared to uncover additional information as you delve deeper.

If you find that you have done your due diligence in the pre-assessment but are still encountering opposition, try running through a list of possible explanations to help rule out what may be contributing to the opposition. **The following are a few reasons why clients may not talk or participate in sessions (Straus, 1999):**

1. **Lack of skill:** Review the student's records to make sure you are working with and approaching the child from an appropriate developmental level. In addition, keep in mind that other factors, such as increased anxiety or impulsivity, can also directly impact a child's skill level within a session.

2. **Boredom:** Check to make sure that you are using the most appropriate and interesting materials for the client, as boredom can cause children to disengage from the process. It is also important to keep in mind that, sometimes, a client may appear to be bored when, in reality, they are fearful, anxious, or depressed.

3. **Opposition for its own sake:** Defiance that is exhibited for the mere sake of being defiant is usually observed when working with children who have a diagnosis of oppositional defiant disorder or conduct disorder. It also tends to occur more in talk therapy than expressive therapies. However, if it does come up, just remember that this may be the only way the student knows how to communicate or establish rapport. Continue to introduce the expressive therapies, and as the client gradually begins to participate, you may see more engagement and improved communication as time goes on. In these cases, it often takes more time to establish rapport with the client. Patience is a true virtue here!

4. **Opposition for power:** In these cases, the resistance is all about control. If you can find a way to set limits (out of concerns for safety and respect) while allowing the student to have control over the materials and content used, then you may be more successful. Give the student a voice in determining the course of therapy and how to proceed. Take a back seat, but still provide guidance and support throughout the process.

5. **Feeling trapped:** Sometimes, clients who show resistance do so because they feel trapped and have learned that expressing feelings or even sharing knowledge of their personal lives results in punishment. When this occurs, the root of the issue is fear. Usually, this fear is linked to home and parental conflict, although it can be social as well. To address this issue, your best course of action is to consistently reinforce that the student is safe in each session. Once they trust that they can openly express their feelings (verbally or nonverbally) to you without recourse, then the resistance and opposition will gradually decrease.

By running through each of these possible explanations, you should find one or more areas that address the source(s) of the opposition. Once you determine this information, then you can tailor the program and treatment plan to meet the client's unique needs.

Killing Time

The need to kill time in session is often related to the previous topic of resistance, as students who resist participating in sessions will falter when it comes to initiating a project. Usually, the student is given a fairly clear directive of how to proceed with a project. **The first place to start is simple: Clarify the directive and ask if the student has any questions about how to begin or proceed.** If the answer is no, then wait! Let students know that you are giving them time to develop and process how *they* would like to begin and that you are available to help. After a short period of time with *no* progression at all, then you can probe further.

Some issues to consider when questioning the student include: Is the student capable of completing the directive? Does the student like or dislike the type of media you have presented? If they do not enjoy it, then ask why. This is important information for future treatment planning. For example, if the student is tactile defensive, then it may be a future goal to integrate into the treatment plan. If the student indicates that they "just can't think of anything," then transition to a decision tree or semantic map to help brainstorm ideas.

Not Enough Time

With particular clients, the opposite problem may happen in that you don't have enough time. In some cases, you will find that a client will spend the entire session creating a product. It is easy to become anxious about speeding up the process so that you may have a finished product in the end, but resist this temptation. The *process* of making the product is part of the intervention as well. There are some clients who take multiple sessions to complete one product. This can be the case with art, music, drama, or even writing.

The key is to encourage clients to describe what they have completed thus far and make a note about where they would like to pick up in the following session. Doing so serves as a reminder during the next session if they are off track. You can then begin the next session with a brief review of what was accomplished in the previous session before restarting the project. Another option may be to allow the client to take the project home and return the following session with more of it completed.

Utilizing Silence

Silence is golden. Isn't that what they say? Well, in a therapeutic setting, silence often creates uncomfortable moments, often more so for the counselor than the client. However, when using expressive therapies, silence can be a sign of progress. Don't be afraid to let there be long pauses with no talking. These moments can provide students an opportunity to process their thoughts without outside influences. You might be surprised that even after what seems to be a very long silence, creativity emerges and the child jumps into a project. Art projects are a particular time when silence is something that should be allowed because it can stimulate creativity. After the student has completed the work, you will have the chance to discuss the process, as well as the outcome of the product itself.

Straus (1999) discusses the value of silence in sessions with youth noting that, "When kids don't want to talk, they are typically both bored and degraded by the discussion of their problem" (p. 4). Often, children and adolescents who present to you in school counseling have been a part of some form of traditional talk therapy in the past and might be expecting a similar experience with you. Sometimes, silence is the most beneficial form of therapy or even the only kind of therapy they can do.

Although it can be difficult to manage or curb your own need to "fill the silence," remember that this is *your* issue and not the client's. As your anxiety rises with each minute of silence, you might find yourself wanting to ask questions or encourage conversation, but refrain from doing so. Most of the time, the child or adolescent will start a conversation on their own, but only when *they* are ready. Instead, fill the time with the art-based activities you have planned, and if there is minimal discussion at the end of the session, then that is perfectly appropriate. The act of making the art is integral to the therapy itself!

INCORPORATING OTHER EVIDENCE-BASED THEORIES

There are many different theoretical perspectives utilized by counselors in the educational setting. However, for the purposes of this book, I will discuss two popular forms of counseling because these are the most popular forms utilized in schools: cognitive-behavioral therapy (CBT) and brief solution-focused therapy (BSFT).

Cognitive-Behavioral Therapy

In CBT, the goal is to assist clients in thinking and behaving differently by identifying their negative automatic thoughts and irrational beliefs, and understanding how this internal dialogue contributes to their behavior. One reason that CBT is commonly used in the school system is because of the effectiveness of the intervention model. In particular, when CBT strategies are implemented in the educational setting, research has shown that it is of significant benefit when it comes to improving emotional, behavioral, social, and academic functioning (Kazdin & Weisz, 2003; Wilson, Gottfredson, & Najaka, 2001; Wilson, Lipsey, & Derzon, 2003).

Using CBT in conjunction with the expressive therapies is a matter of application, as the art process lends itself to many flexible approaches. When used in conjunction, these two modalities can help students learn how to identify problems and develop possible solutions by adding the element of visual prompts and guidance. For example, the concept of a volcano can be used as a metaphor to describe the elements that build up to an explosion, and students can begin to define the feeling of anger and identify triggers related to this emotion. Through the use of the "Volcano Drawing" (Stepney, 2010) and subsequent discussions, students can begin to identify various ways of managing their anger, as well as alternative ways of dealing with it in a more constructive manner. Another adaptation of this concept, which is more well-known, involves using a thermometer as a visual guide to help students identify when their "temperature is rising" and how to "cool it down."

Brief Solution-Focused Therapy

Mental health professionals are usually under specific and time-limited constraints when conducting school-based mental health services, which makes it very difficult to incorporate "traditional" talk therapy or alternate theories that require extended sessions. In this respect, BSFT serves as a great option to address students' needs, as it is usually conducted over the course of four to six sessions. In addition, it can be utilized with various populations of students with a multitude of school problems (Jones et al., 2009). At its core, BSFT is a strength-based and client-driven approach that focuses on helping clients identify solutions rather than investigating the root or origin of their problem(s).

The expressive therapies can easily be woven into the BSFT model without causing much of an interruption in the theoretical process. For example, when presenting the "Miracle Question" intervention, in which clients are asked to imagine what life would be like if their problem was gone, you may ask students to draw their answer instead of just verbalizing it. This approach may help certain students "think outside the box" if they are having difficulty developing or defining their answer. Similarly, the use of puppets in the context of play or drama therapy can also be integrated with BSFT and provide younger children with a nonthreatening medium through which they can discuss their problems (Sklare, 2005).

A FEW LAST TIPS

Don't Be Afraid to Join In

Joining in can be difficult for some mental health professionals who have been trained to be "the observer." However, the expressive therapies are unique in that joining in tends to build rapport and lessens the "threat" of being judged. Often, the first thing you will hear from clients—especially those who are over the age of seven—is something along the lines of, "But I'm not good at drawing." By joining in the activity with them, students can see that there is no judgment in the work itself. Rather, it is the process that is the focus. That being said, this is not always the case, so use your clinical judgment based on what you know about the student, since many students remain self-conscious about participating in expressive therapies.

As children develop, they often go through a phase in which they become self-critical and want their artwork to be "correct" or "perfect," which often leads to abandonment of art altogether. There can also be judgment from peers about the student's skill level, which can come in the form of overtly negative comments or just innocent suggestions (e.g., "You might want to add hair to that girl"). During this phase, embarrassment is often the root of the resistance. In this case, joining in can diffuse the problem and normalize differences in abilities and content choices. This can easily be accomplished through a simple turn-taking directive. For example, you can either start with a scribble and take turns with the student making it into something unique, or give a specific directive (e.g., draw a zoo or amusement park) and take turns creating items to fill the page. Not only is this a great icebreaker, but it also helps to build rapport.

Silence Is Okay

As I mentioned earlier, utilize silence! Don't be afraid to let there be quiet during sessions that include the expressive therapies. Remember, silence often equals creativity. By forcing verbal discussion, you may be interrupting the student's creative process. Even if they are sitting quietly and not engaged in the process at first, they may be thinking about how they want to proceed. You can alleviate the question of whether or not they need help by setting up guidelines in the beginning of your sessions that help them understand that you will not interrupt unless they ask particular questions. You can also provide a nonverbal cue (such as a help card) that is available to them during the creative process. This allows clients to ask for help, even if they are uncomfortable doing so verbally, and it also eases your comfort level in knowing that the option for help is consistently made available through nonverbal means.

However, when has silence gone on too long? Well, I have been in sessions with kids that have not included a single word outside of the greeting, directive, and goodbye. It may be uncomfortable for you, but respecting the student's silence can establish stronger rapport than if you were to force conversation. There is nothing more intrusive than someone interrupting your creative process. When they are finished, they will let you know!

Again, judgment is key in deciding when to ask questions, offer advice, or attempt more engaging conversations.

Remember to Tailor the Medium to Your Client's Needs

Although developing a treatment plan is a standard protocol for all mental health professionals, with the expressive therapies, there is the added component of materials, which is slightly different than traditional therapy models. Many of the expressive therapy techniques can be used for specific purposes, but there are a number of directives that can be used universally. For example, a free drawing or the use of puppets are both fairly universal techniques in that they can be utilized with any school-age child regardless of cognitive ability, diagnosis, or sensory need.

However, always make sure that you keep in mind the child's current mental status, as well as their ability to understand instructions, when considering what types of mediums to use. For example, a student with an aversion to certain tactile input may not respond positively to clay or finger-painting. On the other end of the spectrum, a child who is easily agitated or impulsive will do better with a more controlled medium, such as crayons or colored pencils, than with watercolor or paint. Some of these things you will begin to learn as you experiment with mediums with each client. Most importantly, if you find that you have questions or concerns about a student's progress or mental health status, always seek guidance from a colleague, mentor, or supervisor to discuss the specific case and how to move forward.

Ultimately, though, when it comes to materials, the final decision should always lie with the student. The preference menu discussed earlier can help you decide on the most appropriate mediums. For clients who are able to articulate their comfort level, make sure to have that conversation. Ask them what materials they like to use and why. If they have not worked with a particular medium before, allow them access to it, but watch for indicators of agitation, including escalating behaviors or a refusal to participate.

Whatever the medium, just ensure the student is comfortable with it before you begin. If you see that they are beginning to get uncomfortable or shutting down, move back and try using a different medium or directive. Always be willing to shift gears and let the client drive the direction of the session. Honor each client's unique desires and preferences for specific mediums, and always offer variety in case they would like to expand or try something different.

Infuse Mindfulness Activities

Mindfulness is a tool that is often used in conjunction with the expressive therapies because it allows clients to be present in the here-and-now. By introducing activities such as mindful meditation and guided visualization, you help clients "tune out the noise" and focus on being in the moment during the session. Often, you will notice that after introducing these techniques for a few sessions, clients will begin to ask for mindfulness activities or remind you if you forget to start or end with these activities.

When introducing mindfulness to children, I tell them that it is about recognizing any thoughts and feelings that come and go in their mind, releasing them, and then bringing themselves back to the present moment. I find that it is helpful to start by asking them to list all the things they were thinking about before they came in the room. Then, I explain that mindfulness, or mindful meditation, is meant to help them store those thoughts away for a bit so that they can focus on what we will be doing today. For younger children, mindful meditation can be explained in the simplest manner by asking them to focus on what is happening *right now* in the present moment. Not thinking about what they just did in class or what is coming next after they leave session, but being *here*.

Guided visualization is a little different from mindful meditation in that instead of being present with their thoughts, children use their imagination to visualize a place of relaxation and calm. This is a great tool to use when children are feeling overwhelmed or anxious, or if they aren't familiar enough with mindfulness yet to practice mindful meditation. By using imagination as their guide, children can relax, unwind, or even find joy or peace when they are feeling upset. Guided visualization can actually change the way they are feeling and what they are focused on, which, in turn, helps redirect the focus to the present activity.

Usually, guided visualization is done by reading a script to the child or playing an audio recording. The child finds a comfortable spot, and their only job is to sit or lay quietly while listening to the script and imagining what they are hearing. There are many free scripts available online by googling "free guided visualization for kids."

Decide What Format Works Best

As you continue developing the client's treatment plan, it is also important to focus on the format of the sessions, as the directives will fall into one of three categories: individual, co-experiences, or group.

Individual

Using the expressive therapies in individual sessions is a powerful way to bridge the gap between emotions and words for clients. Individual sessions are more personalized and allow for a specific focus on or expansion of a client's personal needs, which may be more beneficial for children or adolescents who require a platform for processing personal issues. Individual sessions also allow for greater confidentiality, which may be beneficial in a number of different ways with specific clients. For example, children and adolescents who are very private and reserved may not engage as easily in a group setting as they would in an individual session. Additionally, if clients have a history that they are not comfortable sharing with others, then they may feel more comfortable opening up and elaborating on personal information in an individual session.

Co-experiences

The process of co-experience involves working alongside your clients in session, which allows them to feel engaged in the process and also not alone. By working *with* students, you show that you are attempting to work with them to create, as opposed to just "watching." For example, the scribble drawing is an experience in which one person starts by scribbling on a page, and then each person takes turns adding to the drawing to create a full piece of art. Co-experiences can be done with group members as peers or with the facilitator of the individual session. As you introduce this format, you will be able to see fairly quickly whether or not it is productive with specific clients. When it is working efficiently, participants will engage more in the activity and discussion. Getting feedback at the end of the session through the use of reflective questions can be helpful in determining whether your clients would benefit from co-experiences.

Group Work

Using the expressive therapies in the context of small groups can be very helpful for children and adolescents who would benefit from peer feedback or opportunities to practice collaboration and problem solving with others in a safe, supportive environment. By working in a group, children can build rapport with their peers and verbalize their emotions with one another, and it tends to act as a support to normalize feelings and thoughts that may have previously been hidden. Additionally, skill-building opportunities are easily incorporated into group sessions, as children can learn and practice skills in real time with their peers.

Each of these formats can be used interchangeably during treatment, and you will find that many of the directives included in this book will allow you to modify for this flexibility.

Chapter **4**

Art and Drawing Directives

DEVELOPMENTAL PROGRESSION OF CHILDREN'S ART

When using expressive therapies within the context of school-based counseling, it is important to understand that students function at various stages of development when it comes to art. Although most counselors understand that cognitive, emotional, and other developmental milestones differ as a function of child development, there is also a developmental progression to children's art that needs to be taken into consideration when planning and introducing activities.

Why is it important to understand the developmental stages of children's art? Understanding these developmental stages enables you to become more familiar with a child's drawing skills, which allows you, as the counselor, to select appropriate materials and better develop a treatment plan. By tailoring the treatment plan to students' specific ability level, you make sure not to over- or under-challenge them, which ultimately allows them to have *fun* and enjoy the experience.

Although different theoretical models have been used to describe the developmental progression of children's art, each model includes the same trajectory of development, which progresses from *scribbling* to *realistic drawing*. For the purpose of this book, the specific steps in this developmental trajectory are labeled as: (1) scribbling, (2) pre-schematic, (3) schematic, and (4) realistic. Within each of these four stages are substages identified by Cay Drachnik (1995), which help detail the development progression. The chart on the following page details the elements you may find in drawing at certain ages.

Broadly speaking, the progression of these stages occurs between 18 months and nine years of age, although counselors should exercise caution when attempting to interpret ages and stages, as a number of factors can interfere with or influence a child's artistic ability. For example, children are unlikely to progress to the later developmental stages if they lack the necessary resources to help foster their artistic capabilities, such as adult support and educational opportunities (Roland, 2006). In addition, overlap between stages is common. You may see two stages in one drawing, or a child may regress before progressing to the next stage (Roland, 2006).

Scribbling

Scribbling is the universal stage for all children, as all children begin with scribbling regardless of external factors or influences (Roland, 2006). This stage usually begins between 18 months and one and a half years of age with the **random scribble**, in which children show no specific goal but draw uncontrolled lines about the paper. Around one and a half to two years of age, this progresses to a **swing scribble**, which is characterized

CHART I
A Composite of Developmental Levels in Children's Art

ART DEVELOPMENT	ART PRODUCTIONS
1 TO 1½ YEARS **RANDOM SCRIBBLE** 1. Uncontrolled scribble 2. Lacks eye-hand coordination 3. Pounds and pinches clay	
1½ TO 2 YEARS **SWING SCRIBBLE** 1. Beginning of visual motor control 2. Child waves crayon back and forth on the paper in a push-pull motion. 3. Can make snake-like coil in clay.	
2 TO 2½ YEARS **CIRCULAR FORM** 1. The child is emotionally bound up with its mother (circle is feminine). 2. The child will make a ball with clay.	
2½ TO 3 YEARS **THE VERTICAL AND HORIZONTAL** 1. The beginning of figure-ground relationships 2. Vertical line represents the first man. 3. The child starts to name his scribbles and clay products.	
3 TO 3½ YEARS **SUNS AND SHAPES** 1. Crossed lines indicate early attempts to clarify sexual role. 2. Child draws shapes with crossed lines or rays. 3. Pokes and makes decorative forms with clay.	
3½ TO 4½ YEARS **THE FIRST FIGURE** 1. Draws a head with stick-like arms and legs. 2. Has the ability to control his shapes. 3. Can make triangles, crosses, circles and square shapes on paper and with clay.	
4½ TO 6½ YEARS **SCHEMATIC DEVELOPMENT** 1. Can perceive symbols in motion on a line. 2. Uses color realistically. 3. Makes up stories about his drawings. 4. Generally uses the same symbolic form for the same subject each time.	
6½ TO 9 YEARS **LINE AND DETAILS** 1. Child six years old can draw a diamond shape and establish a base line. 2. Uses art as a form of nonverbal language.	
9 YEARS AND UP **DEPTH PERCEPTION** 1. Can create special depth by over lapping. 2. Can perceive that when shapes get smaller and recede in a picture, they give the illusion of depth. 3. Can draw people and figures in action.	

Reprinted with permission from Cay Drachnik and Abbeygate Press, 2012.

by greater motor control as children use a more controlled back-and-forth motion with the pencil or crayon on the paper.

The scribble progression continues to develop into a **circular form** around two to two and a half years of age as children continue to develop greater coordination and planning. Finally, the scribbling takes on **vertical and horizontal forms**, which demonstrates an emerging sense of figure-ground relationships. At the later stages of the vertical and horizontal forms, the drawings may reflect the first representational drawings of people, especially when children begin to name what they are drawing around two and a half to three years of age.

Cathy Malchiodi (2003) describes this stage as one in which the child enjoys the experiences it provides, which are related to tactile feedback and movement. The act of scribbling is one that provides the child with a sense of accomplishment and happiness. There is no specific knowledge of color choice at this stage, and there is minimal control over the movement in making lines.

Pre-Schematic

Around three to three and a half years of age, children move into the pre-schematic stage, where there is an overlap with **suns and shapes**. These drawings may or may not be labeled, but they clearly represent shapes and certain signs or symbols that the child has encountered. These drawings usually consist of shapes with crossed lines throughout, like a sun. Children also begin to name the items in their drawings and even start to include stories about them at this stage (Malchiodi, 2003). By four years of age, the transition to the pre-schematic stage is made and the **first figure** begins to take shape. The first figure usually starts as a tadpole drawing, which is generally comprised of a circle and four lines (representing arms and legs). As time progresses, children exhibit increasing control over the drawings, and the tadpole eventually begins to take a more human form with hands and feet, as well as facial features, although the body is often not included.

As children approach the end of this stage, they begin to include rudimentary body forms. Heads usually dominate the body and can have great detail, such as the inclusion of eyes, smiles, frowns, and ears. The head is thought to represent the most important body part to children at this age because it is associated with particular activities that children deem important, such as talking and eating (Roland, 2006). During this developmental progression, any objects on the page are often "floating" and may be turned in a variety of directions, with multiple objects in one drawing. Color does not play a crucial role at this stage, as children continue to explore with the materials and colors.

When children are in the pre-schematic stage of development, incorporating verbal communication in the context of expressive therapy is important. Doing so not only helps children develop the language needed to describe the work of art they have produced, but it also helps foster the development of imaginative thinking (Roland, 2006). For example, if children draw a person and then describe it as representing themselves, then you can utilize follow-up questions, such as, "What are you doing in the picture?" or "How do you feel in this picture?"

Schematic

The schematic stage usually begins around six or seven years of age and lasts through approximately age nine, as children begin to develop a sense of self and their place in the world. Malchiodi (2003) identifies this stage as the "development of a visual schema," and it includes increasingly more symbols from their environment and experiences. There is a greater focus on **lines and details**, and various objects and symbols become grounded as children begin to include baselines in their drawings. Human figure drawings move from stick people to more full-bodied forms that incorporate greater detail, such as clothing and body parts.

In addition, children at this stage exhibit an increased understanding of how the world moves around them, and their drawings reflect this. For example, there can be themes within drawings based on symbols and signs that reflect the child's world and personal experiences. Similarly, many children at this stage make up stories about their drawings and are often able to create imaginative worlds, either on their own or with some prompting. Children in the schematic stage also begin using art as a nonverbal form of language wherein color is used realistically.

Another unique aspect of this stage occurs around age five or six, with the emergence of the "X-ray drawing." The X-ray drawing is often done when children want to illustrate what is going on *inside* a particular object, as well as the outside. For example, children may draw a picture of their home, in which the rooms inside are visible, as well as the various pieces of furniture or accessories in the home. This makes the object being drawn seem "transparent," as if one were using an x-ray machine to see inside their house (Roland, 2006).

Realistic

When children are approximately nine years old, they move into this last stage of development, where they begin to display an even greater awareness of their surroundings and environment. In this realistic phase, their drawings begin to include specific details, such as color and detail on people, gender characteristics, or aspects of their environment. They also begin to include more action within their drawings. **Depth perception** emerges as children attempt to represent three-dimensional space within their drawings, as well as shadowing and shading within shapes (Roland, 2006). Colors also play a more predominant role, not only to realistically depict the object that is being drawn, but also as a means of displaying any associated feelings. Given this, introducing a "color/feeling" chart in the context of therapy can be helpful at this stage in learning how the child perceives different colors.

In addition, children in this stage often experience an increased need to make the drawing appear "correct" in terms of details and proportion (Roland, 2006). This concern with detail often leads to self-criticism and disappointment when children begin to view their work as not "good enough." Unfortunately, this self-criticism can cause children to stop experimenting with drawing altogether unless they receive adequate encouragement. As a result, counselors who are working with children in the realistic stage would benefit from introducing art instruction and support. Providing psychoeducation surrounding techniques of art may be helpful if the student is hyperfocused on the product being "perfect." In general, by providing the child with positive messages about the process and not the product, it will often lead to productive conversations and not result in a focus on the aesthetics of the art itself.

Summary

As you begin to use more art in your practice with children, you will see examples of how this developmental progression is demonstrated in the artwork produced. The goal in introducing the developmental characteristics in this chapter is to increase your ability to identify any unusual characteristics that might be well outside of the child's expected development so you can identify any areas that might need to be targeted in the future.

The following pages are filled with different ideas for using art and drawing directives with your clients. When you introduce these directives, the first response you will get from older children and adolescents will more than likely be something along the lines of, "Oh, I am not a good artist," "I'm not very creative," or "I am bad at art." When clients come to you with these views, it usually stems from a misunderstanding of what art can be. Remind your clients that the great thing about art is that skill doesn't matter. It is more than learning fine art techniques and getting things to "look pretty." The key to the expressive arts is engaging in the process and uncovering things about themselves that they may not have been able to see when their "intellectual mind" was in charge. Sometimes, the process may not even include "making" art but reviewing other art pieces or using touch to engage with an art project. Encourage each of your clients to come in with an open heart and mind, and remind them that there is no judgment in any of these directives—it is all about their process.

The Color / Feeling Continuum

Although everyone attributes feelings to certain colors, the specific feelings associated with a particular color differ from person to person. Therefore, to understand how colors may play into your client's artwork, consider developing a color/feeling continuum to use as a reference guide.

Materials

- 8 ½ x 11 or 11 x 14 piece of paper
- Watercolors
- Crayons
- Colored pencils
- Paints
- Pens

Directions

1. Create a list of feelings by brainstorming with the client.
2. Divide another piece of paper into boxes associated with the number of feelings identified.
3. Write a feeling in each of the boxes, and then ask the client to match a color with each feeling by coloring in the box with that color.

Reflection and Discussion Questions

1. What feelings were paired with colors for you?
2. Were your answers surprising?
3. How can you use this color/feeling continuum in the future?

Fine Art Feelings

This activity uses classical art pieces to help children understand how art invokes feelings. By introducing a variety of traditional art pieces that evoke various feelings, it encourages children to begin to see how something visual may connect to their feelings. Additionally, it may be a tool that can be used to introduce theory of mind or perspective because children can identify and discuss what feelings the artist may or may not have been trying to portray in the work.

Materials

- Various prints of famous artists' paintings. Here are a few to start with:
    - *The Starry Night*—Vincent Van Gogh
    - *The Scream*—Edvard Munch
    - *American Gothic*—Grant Wood
    - *Number 18*—Jackson Pollock
    - *San Giorgio Maggiore at Dusk*—Claude Monet
    - *Self-Portrait, 1986*—Andy Warhol

Directions

1. Explain that certain images and colors bring up feelings, memories, or even physical feelings when we see them.

2. Explain that you will be showing the client a number of drawings by famous artists, and asking them to make some notes on a small paper to identify the things associated with each picture shown.

3. Introduce at least three to four works of art.

4. Reflect on the activity using the following questions.

Reflection and Discussion Questions

1. Was it easy or difficult to do this activity? Why?

2. Can you think of ways that images in your environment outside of this room might bring up certain emotions or feelings that you haven't thought about before?

Good Things About Me

Using a growth mindset encourages children to move away from the fixed way of thinking that involves "failure" and encourages learning from mistakes. This activity encourages a growth mindset and positive sense of self through modeling and encouragement by turning "mistakes" into new artistic opportunities.

Materials

- Large piece of paper or a sheet of rolled paper
- Watercolors
- Crayons
- Colored pencils
- Paints or pens
- Magazine clippings
- Craft supplies (e.g., feathers, tissue paper, glitter, etc.)
- Pictures (taken together or brought in from home)

Directions

1. Cut the paper into your desired size.
2. Explain to the client that you will take turns making a drawing together in order to create a masterpiece.
3. Take turns describing one good thing about yourself. Then, use the materials to turn this discussion into a visual piece on the paper (e.g., drawing, pictures, words, etc.).
4. At the start of the activity, you can identify a certain number of things that the client must identify as "good things about themselves" if you find the client needs more specific boundaries or rules.
5. If you find that the client is having a hard time coming up with ideas, a spin on this activity is to have each person identify one good thing about the other.

Reflection and Discussion Questions

1. Was it easy or difficult to describe positive things about yourself?
2. Were you comfortable talking about good things about yourself? Why or why not?

Two-Way Scribble

The two-way scribble is a great directive to introduce the concept of art therapy and help the client see that art does not have to be "perfect" to be effective. In this directive, both you and the child create independent scribbles and then work together to combine the two scribbles into a cohesive drawing. This activity is also a great rapport-building technique because it engages the facilitator and the client on an even playing field, leading to a discussion of what is being drawn.

Materials

- Large piece of paper or a sheet of rolled paper
- Watercolors
- Crayons
- Colored pencils
- Paints or pens

Directions

1. Cut the paper into your desired size.
2. Both you and the client then draw a scribble on the paper at the same time for a minute or two.
3. After each of you finish scribbling, work with the client to develop the scribble into one cohesive picture.
4. This process works best when you build on the client's ideas and ask questions to guide them through the picture development.
5. If you remember the five W's (who, what, when, why, where), then the picture will develop with ease. Use these as questions to guide the client as they work, asking questions along the way to clarify and elaborate.
6. Don't be afraid to give input and ideas when asked, but refrain from forcing ideas or limiting the client's creative ideas.

Reflection and Discussion Questions

1. Was it hard for you to find an image in the scribbles?
2. How did you feel during this activity?
3. Is doodling or scribbling something you think you could do on your own when you are feeling emotionally escalated [or the specific feeling the client is working on]?

Powerful and Powerless Collage

In this activity, clients work to develop themes of power and powerlessness through art to help identify areas within their environment that might contribute to these feelings.

Materials

- Large piece of paper or a sheet of rolled paper
- Crayons
- Colored pencils
- Paints or pens
- Magazine clippings
- Craft supplies (e.g., feathers, tissue paper, glitter, etc.)
- Pictures (taken together or brought in from home)

Directions

1. Cut the paper into your desired size. Alternatively, you can also cut the paper into a shape that symbolizes power for the client.

2. Choose a theme (e.g., area of the client's life) and pose a question:

   - What are the things in your life (or in your world) that are powerful or powerless?
   - What makes you feel powerful or powerless?
   - When do you feel powerful or powerless?
   - What do you have power over in your life?
   - What do you have *no* power over in your life?

3. Use the materials to create a picture that answers these questions and creates a picture about the theme identified. Once finished, use each picture to discuss what was drawn.

Reflection and Discussion Questions

1. What was this activity like for you?

2. Were your answers surprising?

3. Can you think of any ways in which you might be able to tap into these powerful parts of you and your environment when you need them?

If I Were a Superhero

Superheroes are often seen as some of the most powerful, confident images. This activity uses that image as a symbol of the self to facilitate discussion and generate ideas of how we might uncover the power within ourselves. By imagining themselves as a superhero, the client is able to uncover these qualities through a different perspective.

Materials

- Large piece of paper or a sheet of rolled paper
- Crayons
- Colored pencils
- Paints or pens
- Magazine clippings
- Pictures (taken together or brought in from home)

Directions

1. Cut the paper into your desired size.
2. Have the client use the supplies to create a picture on the sheet of paper, using the following prompt: "If I were a superhero, I would…"
3. Once the client is finished, use the discussion questions to reflect on and discuss the picture.

Reflection and Discussion Questions

1. Was this drawing easy or hard for you? Why?
2. Can you describe your picture?
3. What kind of things would you do as a superhero?
4. Are there any things that you included in your picture that you could actually do in your life? If so, what are they?

What Is Your Superpower?

Similar to the superhero activity, this activity asks clients to depict what superpower they would identify with in the form of a drawing. This activity helps children tap into the power of positivity by helping them increase awareness of their perceived strengths (aka "superpowers").

Materials

- 8 ½ x 11 or 11 x 14 piece of paper
- Watercolors
- Crayons
- Colored pencils
- Paints or pens

Directions

1. Have clients use the supplies to draw a picture (or write) on the paper, which answers the following question: "If I had a superpower, it would be…"

2. If clients only write an answer, then ask them to draw a picture of what it would look like if they were using this superpower.

3. Once the client is finished, use the following questions to reflect on and discuss the picture.

Reflection and Discussion Questions

1. Was this drawing easy or hard for you? Why?

2. Can you describe your picture?

3. Why did you choose this superpower?

4. If you could have more than one superpower, would you? What else would you choose and why?

My Superhero Mask

This directive introduces the concept of the difference between who we are around others versus our true version of ourselves.

Materials

- Heavyweight paper
- Mask template
- Watercolors
- Crayons
- Colored pencils
- Paints or pens
- String or yarn
- Paper hole punch

Directions

1. Use the template provided on the following page, or cut a mask out of a heavyweight piece of paper.
2. Ask clients to use the template to create their own superhero mask.
3. The following are some questions for clients to consider in developing their mask:
   - *"What kind of colors would you use?"*
   - *"Would there be a symbol or words on it?"*
   - *"What message would you like the mask to send to people when they see it?"*
4. After clients create their mask, have them punch a hole on each side of the mask and thread the yarn/string though to be able to tie the mask on.
5. Once the client is finished, use the following questions to reflect on and discuss the mask.

Reflection and Discussion Questions

1. Was this easy or hard for you? Why?
2. Can you describe your mask?
3. Why did you choose those specific items for your mask?
4. If you could add more items to make your mask a full costume, what would you add (e.g., cape, uniform, etc.)?

Superhero Mask Template

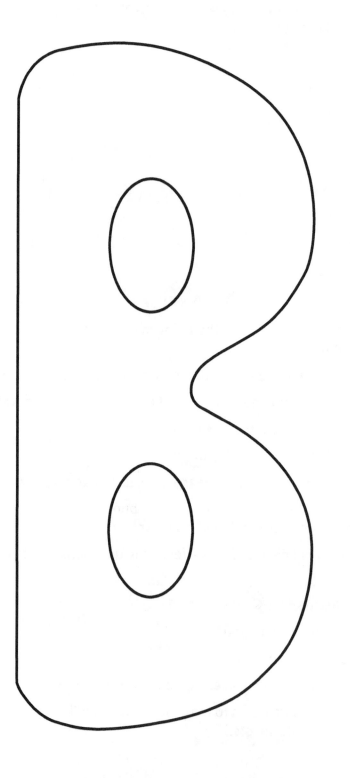

Vision Boards

A vision board is a collage of images that represent the things that clients want in their life. This technique is based on the law of attraction, which states that whatever we focus on is what we attract into our lives. If we harp on that which is negative, then we attract negative experiences into our lives. However, if we send out positive energy, then we receive positive experiences in return. By creating a vision board, clients can work to concentrate on the positive by identifying goals for their future while developing specific steps to meet those goals.

Materials

- 8 ½ x 11 paper or poster board
- Pens and Sharpies®
- Magazine clippings
- Craft supplies (e.g., feathers, tissue paper, glitter, etc.)
- Pictures (taken together or brought in from home)
- Glue, glue stick, Mod Podge® acrylic gloss sealer, or glitter glue

Directions

1. Explain what a vision board is, emphasizing that the images on the board are intended to represent what clients want from life: their goals, dreams, and aspirations.

2. Ask clients to create a list of short-term goals (e.g., friends, school, home) and/or long-term goals (e.g., career, family, future desires) to include on the board.

3. Give clients time to brainstorm and find pictures to include on their board. This may take multiple sessions to complete.

4. If this directive is conducted in the context of a group, clients can share their boards with each other when finished.

Reflection and Discussion Questions

1. What was it like to develop your vision board?

2. Would you be willing to describe your board?

3. What are some specific steps you can take to meet just one of the goals on your board?

Group Photo Collage

Group collaboration on a collage allows clients to identify similarities, navigate social interaction, and build rapport with one another. This directive focuses on group collaboration and helps identify the roles that people naturally take in a group.

Materials

- 8 ½ x 11 or larger piece of paper
- Pens and Sharpies
- Magazine clippings
- Craft supplies (e.g., feathers, tissue paper, glitter, etc.)
- Pictures (taken together or brought in from home)
- Glue or glue stick

Directions

1. As a group, ask clients to decide what size piece of paper they would like to use.

2. Ask clients to create a collage of the group by simply stating, "Create a collage of the group." Try to keep the instructions as vague as possible in order to allow for creativity. If the group requires more structure and boundaries, then you can change the direction to the following instead: "Use pictures to describe what the group means to you."

3. When the group finishes creating their collage, have the clients share their work of art as a group.

Reflection and Discussion Questions

1. What was it like to develop this project with such minimal direction?

2. Would someone be willing to describe your process?

3. How did you come up with the idea for the collage?

4. What kind of things did you learn about yourself while working on this collage?

Free Drawing

This directive simply asks clients to engage in free drawing, without providing them with any specific direction. Often, a free drawing can be either intimidating or liberating to clients. It will usually allow some clients to feel success as they choose to draw something that they know they are "good" at drawing. However, for others, it can feel a bit overwhelming, and they may be hesitant to share either their ideas or skills. It can also give you an idea of their frame of mind and what topic might be on their mind at that time.

Materials

- 8 ½ x 11 paper or larger
- Watercolors
- Crayons
- Colored pencils
- Paints or pens

Directions

1. The directive here is easy. Simply instruct clients: "Draw whatever you want!"

2. After the client finishes their drawing, the discussion should focus on describing the drawing and how it felt to complete it.

   - Don't be alarmed if there is not much discussion. Often, the process of making the art is the therapeutic intervention for the client.

   - You may also not see the effects of this directive in the course of a single session. However, if you save each free drawing, date it, and create a book, then it provides a great documentation of progress to discuss as the counseling continues.

Reflection and Discussion Questions

1. Was this easy or hard for you? Why?

2. What did it feel like to do the drawing?

3. Can you relate what you created to something that is going on in your life right now?

Timelines

Timelines are a great activity to help give clients (and counselors) perspective about specific events in a person's life, as well as how that person views those events. They can be used individually or in a group to allow clients to gain perspective on events or patterns in their lives and to create short- or long-term goals in the future.

Materials

- 11 x 14 paper or larger
- Watercolors
- Crayons or colored pencils
- Paints or pens
- Magazine clippings or pictures

Directions

1. Identify a specific period of time with the client to include on their timeline (e.g., lifespan, calendar year, school year).

2. Once the time period has been established, ask the client to create a timeline with important dates marked within that time period.

3. Have the client use art (e.g., drawing, painting, collage, etc.) to describe each of those dates. The art can represent feelings associated with those dates, specific descriptions of what happened during that time, or anything else that comes to mind.

4. With clients who are anxious or depressed, it can be particularly helpful to also include future dreams on the timeline. Doing so can help reorient the client and assist them in developing a positive outlook about what is to come.

Reflection and Discussion Questions

1. Is there anything that surprised you about what you included?

2. Do you see any patterns in your timeline?

3. What did you include in your future that you are looking forward to? How can you develop some short-term goals to get there?

Road Map

This directive helps clients visualize their goals, as well as the direction they need to take in order to achieve those goals. This activity can be particularly useful for clients who may have trouble verbalizing what it is that they want to achieve and how they can go about doing so. By creating a tangible road map for their short- and long-term goals, clients can formulate ideas about how they may want to create more specific steps, as well as identify possible challenges they may encounter along the way.

Materials

- 11 x 14 paper or larger (turned horizontally)
- Watercolors
- Crayons or colored pencils
- Paints or pens
- Magazine clippings or pictures

Directions

1. Instruct clients to think about a goal that they have in mind to include on the road map.
2. After identifying a goal, have clients draw a road with a beginning and an end on the sheet of paper. Ask them to write their goal at the end of the road, with today's date at the beginning of the road.
3. Ask clients to start at the end of the road and think of what would need to happen *right before* the end goal in order to accomplish that goal. Working backward, ask clients to determine each subsequent step needed to achieve this goal. For example, if their goal is to buy a car, working backward might include:
   - Shopping for a car when they hit their financial goal
   - Saving that percentage each month
   - Calculating what percentage of their paycheck they need to save each month to get to their goal
   - Finding a job(s) that pays
   - Deciding on a new or used model
   - Researching the make and model of the car, including price

Reflection and Discussion Questions

1. What was your goal?
2. Why did you choose that goal?
3. How easy or hard was it to come up with the goal?
4. How easy or hard was it to come up with the road map to meet the goal?

Bridge Drawing

Bridge drawing can be used as a tool to help a client see their past, present, and future. This directive allows the client to see their journey in a concrete form with images that may not be directly related to their idea of the experience.

Materials
- 8 ½ x 11 paper
- Watercolors
- Crayons
- Colored pencils
- Paint
- Pens

Directions
1. To start this exercise, give clients the following directive: "Draw a bridge going from one place to another."
2. The drawing should include an arrow to indicate the direction of travel across the bridge and a dot (representing the client) on the bridge. The dot represents where clients view themselves with regard to a particular goal, situation, or challenge. The arrow represents the client's direction of travel with regard to that current situation.
   - Past: ←
   - Future: →
3. After the drawing is complete, ask the client to describe the bridge and to answer questions about:
   - Where the client came from
   - What is happening now
   - Where the client is going
4. Some other things to consider in this directive:
   - What the client has drawn under the bridge (threatening or non-threatening)
   - Where the emphasis is on the drawing itself (past/future or the bridge itself)

Reflection and Discussion Questions
1. Were you surprised by any part of the directive?
2. What do you think needs to happen to get you to the other side of the bridge?

Adapted from Stepney (2010)

Masks

The purpose of the mask directive can be one or two directional, depending on how you choose to format the treatment plan. You can either ask clients to decorate the inside of the mask or the outside of the mask. By decorating the *inside* of the mask, clients are thinking about how they describe themselves—that is, the characteristics and descriptors that make up who they are. In contrast, by decorating the *outside* of the mask, clients are thinking about how they believe others see them and how they project themselves to the world.

Materials

- Heavyweight paper or papier-mâché
- Paint
- Craft supplies (e.g., feathers, tissue, glitter, stickers, etc.)
- Sharpies
- Glue or glue sticks
- String or yarn
- Paper hole punch

Directions

1. Use the mask template provided on page 42, or cut a mask out of a heavyweight piece of paper. If you have more time, you can also utilize papier-mâché to create a personalized mask.

2. Ask clients to use the paper (or papier-mâché) to create their own mask. Then, move on to decorating the mask. You can either ask clients to decorate the inside of the mask or the outside, depending on the specific treatment goals.

3. After clients create their mask, have them punch a hole on each side of the mask and thread the yarn/string through to be able to tie the mask on.

4. When conducted in a group format, an alternate directive is to have clients create the inside of the mask and pair with another person in the group, who will create the outside of the mask for them. Doing so can help clients gain a perspective of how others view them.

Reflection and Discussion Questions

1. Do you ever show others the inside part of your mask? If so, who do you trust to see it and why?

2. Do you think the people who are closest to you would agree with the outside part of your mask? What makes you think that?

Mandalas

A mandala (which is translated from Sanskrit to mean "circle") is a geometric design, typically in the shape of a circle, which represents wholeness and unity. Mandalas allow clients to contain the drawing, often giving them a sense of calm and control. In addition, the circle is a universal sign of continuity and closure, which often leads to a sense of balance and peace.

Materials

- Mandala template
- Paints
- Pen
- Colored pencils
- Pencil
- Crayons
- Watercolors

Directions

1. Using the mandala template provided on the following page, ask the client to create either an abstract (shapes and colors) or representational (identifiable picture or scene) piece of work within the circle.

Reflection and Discussion Questions

1. Describe your mandala.
2. Was there a reason you chose what you did?
3. How did it feel to draw it?

Adapted from Kellogg, MacRae, Bonny, and DiLeo (1977)

Mandala Template

Coloring Mandalas

Coloring has a calming effect, and pairing it with mandalas is a way to help distract, calm, and refocus attention in order to move into different discussions. By using a predrawn mandala, it alleviates the need for development of the drawing inside the circle. The simple act of coloring is the focus to reduce anxiety and increase a sense of peace and tranquility.

Materials

- Predrawn mandalas
- Pens
- Colored pencils
- Crayons

Directions

1. Use the predrawn mandalas on the following pages, which you can copy for use with your clients. Alternatively, you can find a mandala coloring book of your choosing.

2. Ask clients to spend some quiet time, with or without calming music, coloring the mandala.

3. Instruct clients to pay attention to how they are feeling before and after the exercise. Consider using a 1–5 Likert scale to rate feelings pre- and post-coloring (e.g., 1 = *tense*, and 5 = *calm*).

Reflection and Discussion Questions

1. Was there a reason you chose the design that you did?
2. How did it feel to color it?

Worry Stones

Anxiety and stress are often infused in our clients' daily lives and a topic that comes up in many counseling sessions. In many cultures, worry stones are thought to relieve stress. A worry stone is a smooth stone that fits in the palm of your hand. Rubbing the smooth area of the stone with the index finger and thumb is thought to reduce stress and anxiety.

Materials

- FIMO® soft clay (various colors)
- Oven
- Mod Podge acrylic gloss sealer
- Paintbrush
- Rolling pin

Directions

1. Have clients choose one or two colors of clay for this directive. Instruct clients to roll the clay into a ball and then press it down with their thumb to create a smoother stone.
2. Bake the stone at 230°F on foil for two hours.
3. Once the stone is finished baking, remove it from the oven and have clients paint it with gloss sealer to create a shiny and smooth finish.
4. Whenever clients are experiencing worry, they can hold the stone between their index finger and thumb, and rub it to feel calm.

Reflection and Discussion Questions

1. When do you think you might use the worry stone?
2. Can you think of other items you might be able to turn into a worry stone?

My Iceberg

This directive introduces clients to the idea that behaviors are like an iceberg: Although we can only see the tip of the iceberg, there is much more hiding underneath. Our visible behaviors are on the surface for the world to see, but there are also underlying feelings hidden underneath the water. This is the part of our iceberg that people can't see but that still exists, and it is the driving force behind our behaviors. By developing their own iceberg, clients learn that in order to understand behaviors, it is important to look at the bigger picture.

Materials

- Iceberg template
- Pens
- Colored pencils

Directions

1. Using the iceberg template on the following page, ask clients to use the space above the water to write or draw things about themselves that other people see. These are behaviors that are visible to others, such as anger, irritability, behavior outbursts, or anxiety.

2. Brainstorm with clients to come up with other aspects about themselves that others may not be aware of, usually feelings such as shame, guilt, sadness, etc. Have clients write or draw these things underneath the water.

3. Once clients have finished their iceberg, use the following questions to discuss and reflect on the exercise.

Reflection and Discussion Questions

1. Was this activity easy or difficult? Why?

2. Why do you think it is helpful to know what is under the iceberg?

3. Do you think it would surprise people around you if they could see what is under your iceberg?

Iceberg Template

This is what you see

But if you *really* knew me...

Blooming Positivity

Often, clients will start and sustain a negative thought loop (rumination) that can generalize to other areas of their lives. The field of positive psychology has supported the idea that breaking this thought pattern through the use of gratitude and positive thinking can transform clients' overall general attitudes, leading to a happier state of being. Helping clients focus on the positive increases their gratitude and overall sense of hope, which lends to the development of coping strategies for more challenging situations.

Materials

- Flower template
- Pens
- Colored pencils
- Crayons

Directions

1. Using the flower template on the following page, ask clients to come up with six positive self-statements. These can include statement starters such as:
   I am good at..., *One thing I like about myself is...*, or *People tell me that one thing they like about me is...*

2. Instruct clients to write one statement on each petal.

3. When they are complete, fold the petals into the center of the flower.

4. Whenever a negative thought enters their mind, clients can open each petal and repeat each positive self-statement to themselves until the flower is fully open.

Reflection and Discussion Questions

1. Was it easy or difficult to come up with positive statements about yourself? Why?

2. Where can you keep this flower to use when you need it?

Flower Template

My
Blooming
Thoughts

Magazine Collage

The purpose of this collage is to increase clients' self-awareness and allow them to further explore their feelings about a specific subject. This may be a personal event in their history, or if you are in the rapport-building stage, it may be learning about a specific subject of interest to the client or something neutral about them (e.g., things they like to do for fun). Clients can create their collage with copies of personal photos, magazine clippings, or any personal drawings they have created.

Materials

- Construction paper
- Glue or glue sticks
- Scissors
- Magazine clippings, photos, or drawings

Directions

1. Provide clients with a piece of construction paper, scissors, glue, and an assortment of pictures or magazine clippings that include a variety of topics (e.g., people, places, things, words, letters, etc.).

2. Instruct clients to find pictures that appeal to them and to relate these to a particular topic or directive. The following are some directives you may want to consider including:

    - Biography of someone else
    - Autobiography
    - Collage of a specific feeling or event
    - Free collage (just ask clients to create whatever they want)

3. Once clients have finished looking through the pictures or magazine clippings, have them use their chosen items to create a collage.

4. Discuss the final product by asking clients to describe why they chose particular pictures.

Cautionary Note: I learned early on to tear pages out of the magazines and present them in free form. Otherwise, you will have clients reading the magazines and not completing the activity!

Reflection and Discussion Questions

1. What do the pictures on your collage represent?
2. Why did you choose these particular pictures?

Narrative Drawing

A narrative drawing is a therapeutic intervention that allows clients to put their thoughts about a particular incident or event into a visual format. Drawing out the experience alleviates the pressure of the written word and allows clients to recreate the experience in a nonthreatening format. More than likely, you will know the history of the incident, but this exercise gives clients a chance to share their perspective without feeling judged. Clients experience therapeutic relief as they move away from viewing the event from only their perspective to sharing the perspective of another person, or as they begin to identify the factual pieces associated with the event.

Materials

- Construction paper
- Glue or glue sticks
- Scissors
- Magazine clippings

Directions

1. For this exercise, simply ask the client to "Draw what happened" or "Draw what you remember" regarding a specific incident or event.

2. After the drawing is complete, ask the client to describe the *drawing* itself (*not* the incident that the drawing represents).

3. If clients are unhappy with the outcome, you can also ask them to draw a second picture with the following directive: "Draw what you wish would have happened." Doing so often leads to a problem-solving discussion and facilitates the development of future goals.

Reflection and Discussion Questions

1. Which part of this directive was easier for you to draw?

2. Can you use your drawing to help you find a way to problem solve the issue?

3. If you were to change the story in one way, how would you change it?

Adapted from Malchiodi (2008)

Life on an Island: Group Mural

Group murals are a wonderful way to begin group sessions. They provide a way for the group to get to know each other and give the facilitator a bird's-eye view of how the group interacts. This provides an opportunity to see who may naturally step up as leaders versus followers, as well as how they handle conflict or collaboration differently. Overall, group murals are great directives to use when the group is new or they are having some difficulty engaging in interaction with each other. If conflict does arise, it gives the facilitator an opportunity to use that as a discussion point for processing and problem solving.

Materials

- Paper (2–4 feet)
- Pens
- Pencils
- Colored pens or pencils
- Paint & paintbrushes
- Magazine clippings

Directions

1. Ask clients to create a mural based on the theme "Life on an Island," using whatever medium you have identified (e.g., paint, drawing, collage).

2. When creating the mural, clients should consider the following questions:
   - Where is the island located?
   - How does it look?
   - Who lives on the island?
   - What do they need to survive?

3. Upon completion, ask the group to come up with a name for the island and title it.

Reflection and Discussion Questions

1. What was the process of creating this mural like for you as a group?

2. Was it easy or hard to answer all those questions together? Why?

3. How did you feel about the final product you all created?

Adapted from Stepney (2010)

The Selfie Project

Selfie pictures are part of the societal vocabulary. This group activity uses the mainstream concept of the "selfie" to help clients understand how others see them. This directive gives clients a different perspective because a traditional selfie is created and posted to gain "likes". However, when using art to create your selfie, it is not a "Photoshop®" creation. It allows each member to present aspects of themselves that are not visible in a traditional picture, which also gives peers an opportunity to get to know each other, find similarities, and create connections.

Materials

- Paper (2–4 feet)
- Pens
- Pencils
- Colored pens or pencils
- Post-it® notes

Directions

1. Begin by reviewing what a "selfie" is with the group.

2. Ask clients to use the materials provided to draw a selfie that describes something they like about themselves (e.g., something they like to do, a hobby they have, etc.).

3. Ask clients to write a short description under their selfie, and have them post it on the wall so that everyone's selfies are visible around the room.

4. Ask each client to do an art walk and use Post-it notes to make positive comments about each of the selfies in the room.

5. Come back together as a group and use the following questions to discuss the exercise.

Reflection and Discussion Questions

1. What was the process of creating a selfie like for you?

2. Was it easy or hard to come up with your selfie? Why?

3. How did it feel to read the Post-it notes that people left for you?

The Garden of Self: Group Mural

This directive is great for group collaboration and understanding how to work as a group. It allows the group to get to know each other and provides an opportunity to practice collaboration differently.

Materials

- 11 x 14 paper (turned horizontally)
- Pens
- Pencils
- Colored pens or pencils

Directions

1. Begin by introducing the following garden concepts that clients will use in the creation of their mural:

   - Healthy plants: These represent clients' strengths, or positive situations, that help them grow.

   - Choking weeds: These represent the challenges that clients experience, which may inhibit growth.

   - Seeds: These represent clients' future goals and what they hope to achieve.

2. Give each client their own piece of paper, and ask each client to draw or paint their own garden with these garden concepts in mind.

3. Once everyone is finished, ask clients to line up their drawings on the wall to make one large garden.

4. Discuss how although one person's garden might need more help than another's, we can nurture and help the others grow as a group.

Reflection and Discussion Questions

1. What was the process of creating this mural like for you as a group?

2. Was it easy or difficult?

3. How did you feel about the final product you all created?

Adapted from Stepney (2010)

Zoo Life: Group Mural

As with other group murals, this directive is great for group collaboration and understanding how to work as a group. It provides each member an opportunity to share personal stories and ideas, as well as to work collaboratively with other members to problem solve. As a variation, you can also use the theme of "Under the Sea" instead of the zoo.

Materials

- Paper (2–4 feet)
- 8 ½ x 11 paper
- Pens
- Pencils
- Colored pens or pencils

Directions

1. Provide each client with an individual 8½ x 11 piece of paper and ask them to draw or paint their favorite zoo animal.

2. Post a large mural-size paper on the wall and describe how even though there may be different animals at the zoo, they all live together in one place.

3. Ask the clients to work together as a group to draw or paint a picture of the zoo on the large mural-size paper.

4. Once the picture of the zoo environment is finished, ask each client to cut out their animal and glue it onto the mural.

5. Discussion may be centered around how participants felt during the process, as well as any similarities and differences among the drawings that people found as they worked together.

Reflection and Discussion Questions

1. What was the process of creating this mural like for you as a group?

2. Was this process easy or difficult for you?

3. How did you feel about the final product you all created?

Chapter **5**

Music Directives

J ust like the visual arts, the use of music in the expressive therapies does *not* require that clients (or you) be a musician by trade. Even if clients don't read music or play an instrument, everyone has a musician inside of them. We all have physical rhythmic patterns that our body follows in order to function, and even clients who say they "can't keep a beat" can usually follow some type of rhythmic pattern.

Like art, music can be used as a tool to help clients engage in the therapeutic process and bypass their natural tendency to react to certain situations in an unhealthy manner. Using music with clients allows you to interact with them on a level that doesn't feel forced or prescriptive, like talk therapy can for some. Many times, emotions that have been hidden or suppressed will come to the surface with music, and although this can be overwhelming, it can also be liberating.

Unlike some of the other expressive arts, most people have had *some* exposure to music in their lives, whether they play an instrument or just enjoy listening to it. Even if they have just been exposed to music through others but often don't listen to it themselves, music is an equalizer and is easy to introduce in this sense. When introducing music in the context of the express therapies, you might want to start by just asking clients what their experience with music has been like. You can then choose from some of the following directives, but most of all have fun with it!

Drumming to the Beat

Drumming is an activity that can be done individually or with a small or large group. It is often used to teach rhythm and group collaboration. Keeping rhythm when drumming can create a peaceful grounding feeling that can increase focus and attention, as well as decrease emotional escalation.

Materials

- Drums (one for each client)

Directions

1. The activity can be done in a call and response format (e.g., "I drum one time and then you follow my lead and drum one time"), or the facilitator can hold a beat while clients keep a different rhythm or experiment (e.g., fast/slow, loud/soft).

2. The facilitator can use a mixture of directives with drumming based on the need for an increase in energy in the group (faster responses) or a decrease in energy (slower responses).

3. Vary the responses with each round, asking clients to take turns creating a different call and response pattern.

Reflection and Discussion Questions

1. What was the experience like for you?

2. Was it hard to follow the pattern?

Musical Art

Music and art go together like peas and carrots! Using the two together is a great way to help people who might feel hesitant to use one or the other in isolation feel more comfortable. This group exercise is a take on musical chairs but without the removal of a person in each round. It asks each person to build on the other's artwork while working to music, ending with their own drawing.

Materials

- Paper
- Pens
- Colored pencils or pens
- Music that can be stopped and started

Directions

1. Have clients sit around a table, or in a circular setting, and give them each a blank piece of paper and set of pencils or pens.
2. Play a short segment of a song, and instruct each student to draw until the music stops.
3. Once the music stops, have each client move to the seat to their right and continue the drawing that the previous client was working on.
4. Repeat this process until the group has made a full circle. Then, ask clients to discuss their experience and share each drawing that was produced.

Reflection and Discussion Questions

1. What was the experience like for you?
2. Was it hard to work on something that someone else started?
3. How did you build on the work that was already done?
4. Was this easy or uncomfortable for you? Why?

Musical Song

This group directive is similar to Musical Art, but it focuses on song development instead. In particular, it asks each client to create a written work after listening to music. The use of a symphonic or classical piece takes the lyrics away so the client can focus on their own thoughts and ideas.

Materials

- Paper
- Pens
- Colored pencils or pens
- Music (symphonic or classical)

Directions

1. Have clients sit around a table, or in a circular setting, and give them each a blank piece of paper and set of pencils or pens.

2. Instruct each client to write a poem or freestyle song lyric until the music stops.

3. Once the music stops, have each client move to the seat to their right and continue the poem or lyric that the previous client was working on.

4. Repeat this process until the group has made a full circle. Then, ask clients to share their experience and read the song or poem that was produced.

Reflection and Discussion Questions

1. What was the experience like for you?

2. Was it hard to work on something that someone else started?

3. How did you build on the work that was already done?

4. Was this easy or uncomfortable for you? Why?

Beautiful Musical Mess

Sometimes, it is difficult to see the beauty in the chaos around you. By providing clients with an opportunity to create a mess in a way that has an element of structure, clients can come to understand that getting messy doesn't always have to be negative. Finding the beauty in the mess is a great lesson for us all to learn. This directive involves using art and music to create an unstructured painting, which allows clients to recognize the beauty found in the chaos. It can be done in an individual or group format.

Materials

- Paper (large mural size)
- Paint (various colors)
- Paintbrushes
- Music

Directions

1. Provide each client with a paintbrush and a variety of paint colors to use.
2. Ask clients to apply paint to the canvas in different ways (e.g., dripping, splattering, brushing, finger painting, etc.) throughout the course of one song.
3. Instruct them to try to keep painting *without trying to make any images* for the entirety of that song.
4. At the end of the song, ask clients to stop. Spend a few minutes cleaning up, and return together to review.

Reflection and Discussion Questions

1. What was the experience like for you?
2. Was it easy or hard to paint without trying to make an image?
3. Was it easy or hard to keep painting the entire time?

You Write the Song

We all have a story to tell, and sometimes we just need a format to be able to articulate our thoughts and feelings. Song writing encourages clients to create their own story and gives them the opportunity to do so with their desired level of personalization. This activity involves asking clients to develop their own song lyrics, either from scratch or by building on a chosen song. This can be used in a group or individual format.

Materials

- Paper
- Pens or pencils
- Music (if needed)

Directions

1. Give each client a piece of blank paper and a pen or pencil, and ask them to create their own song lyrics from scratch.

2. If clients find it too difficult to create an original song, they can use a favorite song and just change the lyrics to personalize it.

3. Offer time at the end of the session to share the songs that each client created, but don't force anyone to share. Alternatively, you can ask clients to trade songs with each other and have others read their creative works.

Reflection and Discussion Questions

1. What was the experience like for you?
2. Was it easy or hard to create your song? Why?
3. What did you like about the activity?

Find the Emotion

Different types of music evoke different feelings for each of us. One form of music or a specific song may make one person feel happy and nostalgic, while another may feel sad and lonely. Music, emotions, and memories are linked together in some of the strongest forms. Helping people uncover the feelings they have with certain music can lead to more self-awareness in other aspects of their lives as well. It encourages clients to be present and aware of their inner and outer experiences, which promotes emotion regulation. In this activity, clients are asked to evaluate various types of music in order to identify the emotions that each song evokes.

Materials

- Paper
- Pens or pencils
- Music (various types with various lyrics)

Directions

1. Give each client a piece of blank paper and a pen or pencil.

2. Explain to clients that they will be listening to different types of music, and their task is to listen to the lyrics in order to identify what feelings or emotions the songwriter may have been experiencing when writing the song.

3. After the last song is played (you determine how many based on your session time) review the group responses.

4. A variation on this directive is to have clients focus on how the music makes *them* feel (as opposed to the songwriter). If you are using the same songs as you did in the previous steps, then you can ask the group to compare their previous responses to see if their feelings are the same or different from what the songwriter wrote or intended. If clients find that lyrics are distracting, then you can also consider using instrumental music for this variation.

Reflection and Discussion Questions

1. What was the process like for you?

2. Was there a difference in how you felt each time you listened to the lyrics?

3. Did any of the songs make you think of a memory from your past?

Feeling the Song

This directive asks clients to begin thinking about how emotions are associated with the lyrics in their favorite songs and how music directly relates to feelings. By introducing clients to the notion that music is linked to our emotions, they can begin using music as a coping tool to change or transform their moods and negative thought patterns.

Materials

- Paper
- Pens or pencils
- Music

Directions

1. Give each client a piece of blank paper and a pen or pencil.

2. Ask clients to identify one song that may relate to their experiences and/or current situation, and have them write the lyrics to that song on a piece of paper.

3. Direct them to focus specifically on the lyrics of the song and how the words made them feel, making notes on the page next to the lyrics.

4. Ask them to highlight their feelings using two colors to signal either positive or negative emotions.

5. For higher functioning or older clients, you can also ask them to analyze the lyrics either from their own perspective or from the perspective of the musician who wrote it.

6. Open the group for discussion and allow clients to share their experiences.

Reflection and Discussion Questions

1. What was the process like for you?

2. Were there songs that were easier to link to experiences in your life than others?

Shake, Rattle, and Roll

Rain sticks, shakers, and other rattling tools are forms of great fun for young and old children alike. The shakers can be used individually, in a group, and with or without music. This directive involves having clients create make-and-take music shakers. As with drumming, the shakers provide clients with ways to use rhythmic sounds and motion to regulate emotions and ground themselves in the present moment.

Materials

- Cardboard tubes (paper towel or toilet paper)
- Scissors
- Various patterns of washi tape
- Stapler
- Rice, corn kernels, beans, stones, or other small items
- Markers
- Paint

Directions

1. Start off by explaining to clients that they will be creating make-and-take music shakers.

2. Let each client choose a tube and tape to use.

3. Have clients cover one end of the tube with two layers of tape. Before applying the first layer, it is helpful to score it first (like a sun toward the center) in order to make it easier for the tape to form around the tube. Then, add a second layer of tape over the first.

4. Clients can then fill the shaker with a variety of small items of their choosing. Two to three tablespoons generally works best.

5. Have clients seal the other end of the tube using the same method, and ask them to decorate their music shaker as desired.

Reflection and Discussion Questions

1. What was it like to make a music shaker?

2. When do you think you might use this at home? At school?

The Musical Feelings Scale

In this exercise, clients listen to various different songs and describe the emotions associated with these songs using a musical feelings scale. The goal of this activity is to help clients understand the impact that certain types of music have on their mood, behavior, and functioning.

Materials

- Musical Feelings Scale
- Pens or pencils
- List of songs, itemized by number for reference. Make sure to include a variety of genres, ranging from symphonic and jazz to rap or heavy metal.

Directions

1. Provide clients with a copy of the Musical Feelings Scale on the following page.
2. Place the itemized list of songs, which reveals the title of each song and its accompanying number, next to them.
3. Instruct clients to listen to each song as it is presented and to record the feelings associated with that song on the scale provided. To do so, they simply write the number of that song on the line corresponding to the feeling.
   - For example, if the first song is "Jingle Bells" and this song is related to a happy or joyful feeling, then the client would write a number "1" on the line closest to that feeling.
4. Repeat this process until each song is played, and then discuss how the client related these feelings with the songs.

Reflection and Discussion Questions

1. What was the process like for you?
2. Did any of these songs make you recall a memory?
3. What song was the happiest for you? The saddest?
4. Were your answers different than others in the group ("if done in a group format")?

Musical Feelings Scale

Ecstatic Joyful Happy Calm Tired Anxious Agitated Worried Scared Angry Aggressive Furious

Comments/Notes

Musical Notebook

We all have some form of a playlist of our life in our head. Music is a part of our lives from the time we are born, and whether it is a song that our parents played or sang to us, or music we remember from special occasions, emotions are usually linked to the music we remember. In this activity, clients create a notebook with a menu of songs that evoke feelings.

Materials

- Composition book or handmade notebook
- Pens or pencils
- Colored pens or pencils
- Music bank or access to an online music source (e.g., Pandora®, Amazon Music®, etc.)

Directions

1. Provide clients with writing materials and a notebook, and ask them to list at least four feelings (can be more if desired) on the first page of the notebook.

2. Ask them to tab as many areas in their notebook for the number of feelings they listed (e.g., four feelings = four tabs).

3. Explain that clients will search the online or musical database to find at least five to ten songs for each feeling they listed and write these songs in each of the tabs in their notebook. If there is time, you may choose to have clients complete this task in the same session. Otherwise, it can be done either as homework or across two sessions to allow time to gather the music.

4. Under each song, ask clients to make a note about why they chose that song and how it relates to the feeling.

5. Give clients an opportunity to share.

6. Encourage clients to continue adding to their notebook as they find new songs, which they can use to create their own relaxing or uplifting playlist.

Reflection and Discussion Questions

1. Was it hard to find songs for each feeling?
2. Were there some feelings that were harder to find songs for than others?
3. Was this easy or uncomfortable for you? Why?

Follow the Leader

Follow the leader is one way for children to observe another person modeling how to inhibit, self-monitor, and organize their responses. Young children or children who are working toward executive functioning mastery benefit from modeling these skills. This activity involves a call and response style hand-clapping game that builds on itself with a group. This can be done in an individual or group session.

Directions

1. Model a call and response with hand-clapping. For example, "Pat Pat CLAP CLAP... Pat Pat CLAP."

2. Explain that the first person in the group will start with a short one to two pattern response, and the person to the right will repeat that response and then add another one to two responses to it. For example:

   - Person 1: "Pat CLAP."

   - Person 2: Repeats "Pat CLAP," then adds "CLAP CLAP" to create "Pat CLAP... CLAP CLAP."

   - The next person repeats the full sequence and then adds to it as well: "Pat CLAP CLAP CLAP...Pat."

3. The group continues this sequence until it reaches the last person in the group. Then, the whole group tries to complete the sequence together.

Reflection and Discussion Questions

1. Was this easy or uncomfortable for you? Why?

2. How hard was it to remember the sequence?

3. How many pats/claps do you think you could remember at once?

What Color Is Your Music?

Using more than one medium at a time helps clients explore feelings in different ways in order to expand their definitions and experiences with each feeling. This activity uses color and music together to ultimately help clients see that feelings may be multidimensional.

Materials

- Various colored Post-it notes
- Various instruments (e.g., guitar, tambourine, chime, triangle, bongo, harmonica, etc.)

Directions

1. Give each client Post-it notes in various colors.

2. Ask them to write a feeling they associate with each color on the various Post-it notes.

3. Ask clients to match each colored Post-it note with an instrument and sound pattern (e.g., quick beat versus slow beat). For example, they may choose a drum and a fast five-beat pattern for yellow (anxious) and a slower two-beat pattern for blue (sad).

4. Once they have matched a color to an instrument/sound pattern, ask them to line up the Post-its with the corresponding sounds/patterns and play the series of colors for the group.

Reflection and Discussion Questions

1. How did it feel to match the instruments and patterns to the colors?

2. How was it to play the series that you created?

Tissue Dancing

This group activity is a movement version of musical chairs in which clients must practice dancing to music while balancing a piece of tissue paper on their head. It can be used to help clients practice executive functioning skills, such as inhibitory control, as well as following directions.

Materials

- Facial tissue (one per client)
- Varied types of music

Directions

1. Give each client a tissue, and ask them to place the tissue on top of their head.

2. Before turning the music on, let clients know that they need to dance while the music is playing with only one rule: DO NOT LET THE TISSUE HIT THE FLOOR.

3. If the tissue falls off their head, then they may put it back on, but if it hits the floor, then they are out until the next round.

4. The last person dancing wins that round.

Reflection and Discussion Questions

1. Was this easy or uncomfortable for you? Why?

2. How hard was it to keep the tissue on?

3. How did you feel when you got out?

Your True Colors

In this activity, clients use the song "True Colors" by Cyndi Lauper to help drive self-awareness and insight into their own uniqueness by pairing shapes and feelings.

Materials

- Colored construction paper
- Scissors
- 8 ½ x 11 or 11 x 14 paper
- Pens and pencils
- Glue
- The song "True Colors" by Cyndi Lauper

Directions

1. Provide clients with various pieces of colored construction paper. Ask them to choose a few colors that make them feel good. These can be colors that they associate with being happy, calm, safe, or any other positive feeling.

2. Once they have identified some colors of their choosing, have them cut a shape (any shape they desire) out of each color.

3. Listen to "True Colors" and ask the group members to share what it means to them. The underlying theme of the song lyrics speaks to uniqueness, which will be used in the activity.

4. Using the different colored shapes, have clients write down one thing they see about themselves that is unique and special on each shape.

5. Once clients have written something on each shape, have them glue the shapes onto the larger paper (either 8 ½ x 11 or 11 x 14).

6. Give each client an opportunity to share.

Reflection and Discussion Questions

1. Was this easy or uncomfortable for you? Why?

2. Was it easy or difficult to come up with more than one thing that was unique about you?

Song Chaining

Music can be an effective tool to help people connect and bond through a shared musical experience or through the use of music to discuss feelings. In this group exercise, clients create a musical piece by building on each other's music. The creation of a large piece of music through each participant's smaller contribution leads to a communal pride in the final product.

Materials

- A variety of instruments (e.g., guitar, tambourine, chime, triangle, bongo, harmonica, etc.)

Directions

1. Have each client choose an instrument and sit in a circle.

2. Explain that each person is going to come up with a single sound from their instrument and play it continuously.

3. Ask one person to start and continue playing.

4. Instruct the person sitting to the right to add on to the song with either their instrument or a voice tune.

5. Have each client continue this process until everyone in the circle is playing together. For a great review, you can also record the song from start to finish and then replay for everyone.

Reflection and Discussion Questions

1. Was this easy or uncomfortable for you? Why?

2. How did it feel to begin and continue playing?

3. Did you like the final product? Why or why not?

Find the Sounds

Building rapport and trust in a group setting is an important element in facilitating a strong group experience. This activity involves having clients work together to use their auditory discrimination skills to find various sounds around the room. It also forces clients to pay close attention, which gives them an opportunity to practice using selective and focused attention skills.

Materials

- A variety of instruments (e.g., guitar, tambourine, chime, triangle, bongo, harmonica, etc.)

Directions

1. Have the "hider" place various instruments around the room, some of which are easily seen and others that are not easily seen.

2. The "seeker" is blindfolded and sits to listen.

3. The "hider" chooses an instrument and moves to a specific location in the room, where they then play a sound and hide the instrument in that place.

4. The "seeker" takes off their blindfold and moves about the room to find the instrument.

5. This activity can be done individually (between a client and therapist) or in a group format. In a group format, each person would sit next to a different instrument and the "seeker" will determine which instrument was played (matching it to the group member). Each group member can take turns being the "seeker."

Reflection and Discussion Questions

1. Was this easy or uncomfortable for you? Why?

2. What was the hardest instrument to find?

3. What was the easiest instrument to find?

Music and Movement

A good group dynamic helps encourage turn-taking and active listening among group members. This group exercise promotes both skills through a follow the leader task in which clients create a movement that is paired with music.

Materials

- A variety of types of music

Directions

1. Have all the clients in the group join together in a circle.

2. Choose a song and have one client begin the activity by entering the circle and starting a repetitive movement (e.g., swaying their hands back and forth).

3. The group copies the movement until the person in the center taps another group member on the shoulder, signaling a switch.

4. The newly tapped member enters the circle with a new movement that the group then copies.

5. This process continues until all group members have had a turn or the song is over.

Reflection and Discussion Questions

1. Was this easy or uncomfortable for you? Why?

2. How did it feel to be in the middle and lead the group?

Musical Telephone

The game of telephone is an activity that has long been a part of childhood games and can be used to teach clients about the impact that gossip and the relay of messages from a third party can have on a message. This group exercise integrates the classic game of telephone with a musical twist to maintain the message yet change up the format. This activity is best used with groups of five or more.

Materials

- Group members (five or more)

Directions

1. Have all the clients in the group join together in a circle.

2. Choose one person to begin the exercise. That client chooses a song that most people know and whispers the title of the song to the person to the right of them.

3. That person turns to the person to their right and shares the title of the song.

4. Once the musical telephone gets to the last person in the circle, that person sings the first part of the song to the group, and the original person shares whether or not it is correct.

5. Variation: For younger children or children in need of simplicity, you can choose to just sing the song or say the title instead of alternating between the two.

Reflection and Discussion Questions

1. Was this easy or uncomfortable for you? Why?

2. Did you expect that you would get it correct?

3. Have you ever seen a message get changed like this in your life?

Freeze Dance

Freeze dance is a fun group exercise that helps reinforce inhibitory control and body awareness through movement. Adding scarves to the activity allows clients to use them as a focus during their dance and also increases awareness of their personal space between others.

Materials

- Music that can be stopped and started
- Scarves

Directions

1. Instruct each client in the group to choose a scarf and stand up.
2. Explain to clients that when the music starts, they will begin free dancing with their scarves.
3. When they hear the music stop, they will freeze just where they are.
4. Continue with the freeze dance activity for as long as needed during the session.
5. End the activity by having everyone form a large circle and freeze dance in the circle for the last song.

Reflection and Discussion Questions

1. Was this easy or uncomfortable for you? Why?
2. Was it hard to stop when the music stopped?
3. What was your favorite part of the freeze dance?

Soundtrack of Life

Many times, clients do not take time to reflect on how events and experiences have led to the decisions and actions they take in the moment. Music is infused in our lives, at times without us even knowing it. In this activity, clients create songs and a unique and personal CD cover for the soundtrack of their life.

Materials

- Paper
- Paper cut to CD case size
- CD case
- Pens or pencils
- Colored pens or pencils
- Music (if needed)

Directions

1. Ask clients to create a soundtrack of their life by coming up with a list of song titles that describe their life. These can be real songs or made up titles.

2. Once the song list is complete, give each client a CD case and paper, and ask them to create a CD cover for their soundtrack. Encourage them to use their experiences and song choices to guide their images for the CD. It can include pictures, words, or both.

3. Give each client an opportunity to share.

Reflection and Discussion Questions

1. Was this easy or uncomfortable for you? Why?

2. Are there certain times in your life that were harder to find songs for than others?

3. Are there certain songs that you didn't include that you remember from your life? Why didn't you include them?

Your Theme Song

Life can have a theme song, just like movies. We have all had songs in our head at certain times in our lives that help us through difficult situations or remind us of something important or special. This activity, which can be done in either an individual or group format, asks clients to create a theme song for their life.

Materials

- Paper
- Pens or pencils
- Music (if needed)

Directions

1. Discuss what a theme song is by referencing movies and describing how certain songs are linked to theme songs in movies. For example, "You've Got a Friend in Me" from *Toy Story* is used to describe the theme of friendship that is included in that movie.

2. Ask clients to think about what their current theme song might be. It might be a song that describes a difficult time or situation they are experiencing, or one that is associated with a happy or extra special memory or experience. Clients may also find that they have more than one theme song that corresponds with certain parts of their day.

3. Ask clients to take a few moments to write down why they chose this particular song(s).

4. If this activity is being done in a group format, try to help each client find the music online and play it for the group.

5. Once clients are finished, use the following questions to review their song choices.

Reflection and Discussion Questions

1. Was it difficult to choose a song?

2. Why did you choose the song(s) that you did?

3. How does this song (or songs) make you feel when you hear it?

Timelines in Song

Sometimes, it is helpful to create a visual map of our lives in order to gain perspective of where we are today. For this activity, clients create a timeline for a specific period of time in their life (or, if they'd like, their full lifespan) and pair various life moments with songs.

Materials

- Paper (at least 11 x 14)
- Pens or pencils
- Colored pens or pencils
- Music (if needed)

Directions

1. Identify a specific period of time with the client to include on their timeline (e.g., lifespan, calendar year, school year).

2. Once the time period has been established, ask the client to create a timeline with important dates marked within that time period.

3. Ask the client to find a song for each noted date on their timeline and to write it down. The song can represent feelings associated with those dates, specific descriptions of what happened during that time, or anything else that comes to mind.

4. If necessary, use a music database to help clients identify songs.

5. Once the client is finished, use the following questions to review the timeline.

Reflection and Discussion Questions

1. Was this activity easy or uncomfortable for you? Why?

2. Why did you choose the songs that you did?

3. If you had to include future dates on your timeline, what dates would you include and what songs would you choose for them?

Chapter

Play Directives

Play is a natural thing for children (and even adolescents!) to do. The play directives are usually the easiest to introduce and often the most requested in counseling. Although children start to move away from play as they get older because they think that it is "childish," you will find that in their hearts they still love to play. Even adults love to play when they let themselves stop "adulting" for a moment. Given this, don't hesitate to start with the following 24 directives if you find that you have a resistant client, or if you get some initial pushback with the other forms of expressive therapies. You can't go wrong with play!

Discussion Cube

The Discussion Cube is a great tool to use at the beginning of a counseling session, or if a student is just stuck and needs a little game to help start a discussion. In a group format, the Discussion Cube is also a great icebreaker activity. The cube is made up of six different topics written on the sides (e.g., something that scares you, your dream job, something that makes you happy, a place you would like to visit, something that makes you angry, something you wish for) that can be used to stimulate conversation. Clients can take turns rolling the cube, much like dice, and discuss whatever topic they land on.

Materials

- Discussion Cube template
- Heavy cardstock paper
- Color printer
- Tape or glue

Directions

1. Make a copy of the discussion cube template (pg.97) on cardstock paper, cut it out, and assemble it using the following steps:

    - Fold each of the tabs inward.

    - Fold up A and B around C.

    - Fold up D, tucking in the flaps as you go.

    - Fold E over the top.

    - Fold down F.

    - Tape or glue the sides together.

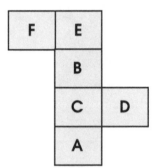

2. Once the cube is assembled, have each client in the group take turns rolling the cube to start the discussion.

Reflection and Discussion Questions

1. Was this easy or uncomfortable for you? Why?
2. What would be some other things you would put on your own discussion cube?

Discussion Cube Template

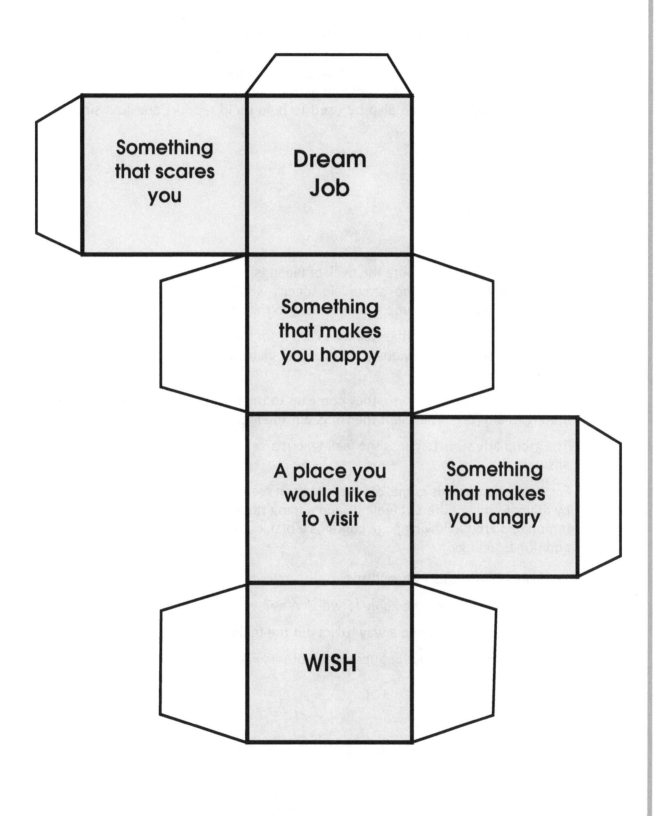

"I Am" Feelings

Feelings cards are a great tool to allow clients to act out their feelings, and identify and discuss how feelings relate to certain situations. Being able to use a format other than talking is helpful because, many times, clients have difficulty attaching words to feelings, but they are able to use play and acting to relay them through an experience. In a group format, the cards can also be used to help build rapport and find similarities among group members.

Materials

- Feelings cards
- Play props (as needed)

Directions

1. Shuffle and evenly distribute the deck of feelings cards (page 99) to each client, or put them in a pile on the "stage." To specify what area of the room is considered the "stage," have a play prop available next to this area.

2. Have clients take turns either taking a card from the community deck or choosing one from their hand (previously shuffled and distributed), and then acting out the feeling on that card.

3. Whenever it is a client's turn, they come up to the stage and act out that feeling by stating, "I am [...]." The client then acts out the feeling without sharing what it is.

4. The group attempts to guess the feeling, but after three tries, the client shares the answer.

5. For a variation on this game, older clients can create their own feelings cards by brainstorming different feelings and adding them to the "feelings deck." The template on the following page contains a blank space where clients can add additional feelings.

Reflection and Discussion Questions

1. Was this easy or uncomfortable for you? Why?

2. Was it hard for you to find a way to act out the feeling card you chose?

3. Was it easier to act it out or guess when others were acting?

Feelings Cards

Happy	Anxious	Sad	Frightened
Angry/Mad	Furious	Worried	Ecstatic
Joyful	Tired	Excited	Overwhelmed
Jealous	Exhausted	Disappointed	

Zones at Work

This activity is based on the "zones of regulation," in which clients are taught to regulate their emotions and behaviors by understanding them in the context of zones: green, yellow, red, and blue (Kuypers, 2011). The first step in teaching clients how to regulate their emotions and behaviors is to help them understand what things in life make them feel escalated or overwhelmed. By playing this game, clients of all ages can get in touch with the external factors that may trigger their emotional reactions and place them in these various zones.

Materials

- Colored construction paper (green, yellow, red, and blue)
- Zones at Work Scenario List (you can create your own list of real-life scenarios)

Directions

1. Place each of the colored pieces of paper around the room, far enough away from each other that clients have to move or walk to get to a different paper.

2. Review the meaning of each of the different colors:
   - Green: happy, calm, and content
   - Yellow: slightly elevated, agitated, or anxious
   - Red: overwhelmed, experiencing difficulty controlling emotions
   - Blue: tired or sad

3. Read from the Zones at Work Scenario List on the following page, or from your own list, and ask the client to move to the color associated with the feeling each scenario invokes.

4. As you move through the examples, pause to discuss why clients chose specific colors and what tools they could use to de-escalate and return to a happy, calm, and content state. Highlight any activities that clients identify as helping them return to the "green," and reinforce these as coping strategies.

Reflection and Discussion Questions

1. What is the color that you feel most comfortable in?
2. What tools do you have to get back to green right now?

Adapted from Kuypers (2011)

Zones at Work Scenario List

- Going to a movie

- Completing homework

- Reading a good book

- Studying for a math test

- Going on vacation

- Finding a spider in your room

- Spending a day at the beach

- Listening to music

- Doodling or free drawing

- Hanging out with your friends

- Listening to an audiobook

- Shopping

- Traveling over a bridge

- Visiting your family

- The first day of school

- The last day of school

- Finding a snake during a walk

- Petting a dog or cat

- Having a substitute teacher

- Teaching someone younger than you how to do something

- Learning a new activity

- Swimming in the pool

- Trying to talk to a friend after an argument

- Asking for help from an adult

- Asking for help from a peer

- Confronting a peer that said something mean to you

- The first day at a new school

- Riding in a car

- Going to a concert

- Eating ice cream

- Going on a walk with a friend

Shadow Skills

In this activity, clients use their imagination to build a shadow box and put on a puppet show. Puppets can be used to tap into imagination and creativity with clients who may have difficulty finding this outlet. It can also be a useful tool in allowing clients to play out scenarios from their own lives without having to verbally talk through them.

Materials

- A cardboard box (a cereal box works well)
- Scissors or utility knife
- Tape
- Thin white paper or wax paper
- Straws, craft sticks, tongue depressors, or skewers
- A light source (a desk lamp works well)

Directions

1. Explain to clients that this activity will involve putting on a shadow puppet show, in which clients may create stories or role-play a real-life scenario from their own experience. For example, they may create a shadow box of a classroom and then recreate various experiences that they have struggled with in the classroom.
2. Tape up the cardboard box to ensure that it is sturdy and closed.
3. Cut out the larger sides of the cardboard box, leaving a 1- to 1 ½-inch border around the edge. Do this on both sides, and save the extra cardboard to make puppets.
4. Check to make sure you don't need to secure the box with more tape.
5. Tape a piece of wax or tracing paper over one side of the cutout to form a screen. This side of the paper will face the audience.
6. Use the leftover pieces of cardboard to draw and cut out images of different puppets. Then, glue the puppets onto sticks.
7. When you are ready for the show, position the side of the box with the screen toward the audience, and shine a light through the back of the cardboard box. Have clients use the puppets or their hands to create the show.
8. You can use topics to create the show or just freestyle it (creating imaginary scenes or stories).

Reflection and Discussion Questions

1. Can you think of other stories you could create with this?
2. Did you like coming up with the stories for your shadow box? Why or why not?
3. What was your favorite part?

Feelings Jeopardy

In this group activity, clients practice identifying various physical sensations associated with the different "zones of regulation" through a jeopardy game format. It can be used as either an introduction to the material or a way to reinforce the skills already learned. This activity can be used with groups of two or more.

Materials

- Jeopardy cards

Directions

1. Review the zones of regulation (page 101), as well as the game of Jeopardy® if anyone is unfamiliar with it.

2. To play the game, use the Jeopardy cards provided on the following page, and remind clients that they must answer in the form of a question.

3. If you have time, ask clients to come up with two to three of their own Jeopardy questions and use them in a second game. An additional blank template is provided for clients to do so.

Reflection and Discussion Questions

1. Was this easy or difficult for you? If so, which part and why?

2. Do you think this activity will make it easier to remember what zone you might be in when you start to feel certain physical feelings?

Jeopardy Cards

___When you are in the green zone, your body feels **THIS**, which is the opposite of tight. Answer: *RELAXED*	You have racing thoughts when you are in **THIS** zone. Answer: *YELLOW*	I am starting to blow my top so I must be entering **THIS** zone. Answer: *RED*
Smiling and being ready to learn means I am in **THIS** zone. Answer: *GREEN*	I might start to cry if I am in **THIS** zone. Answer: *BLUE*	My heart is starting to beat _____ when I am in the yellow zone. Answer: *FAST*
I stop listening and hearing what others are saying in **THIS** zone. Answer: *RED*	I'm not cold, I'm starting to feel **THIS** temperature when I am in the red zone. Answer: *HOT*	I might be _____ (starts with a Y) if I am in the blue zone. Answer: *YAWNING*

Tower Building

This exercise helps clients practice self-control and manage feelings of disappointment and frustration through the process of tower building (and rebuilding). By providing a safe place to practice managing the frustration of the falling tower, clients are encouraged to generalize these positive coping strategies outside of the controlled environment.

Materials

- Large Lego Duplo® blocks or smaller wooden blocks

Directions

1. Prior to starting the exercise, review strategies for managing disappointment and frustration (e.g., deep breathing, taking a break or walk, counting, etc.).

2. Ask clients to build a tower as high as they can, and let them know that the goal is to continue building it until it falls on its own.

3. As the tower gets taller and less stable, or as it repeatedly falls down, point out physical signs of escalating frustration in the client, and demonstrate and encourage the use of the regulation strategies identified in Step 1.

4. If possible, have the client attempt to build and rebuild the tower at least three times.

Reflection and Discussion Questions

1. What part of the building was the easiest? Why?

2. What part of the building was the hardest? Why?

3. Were you able to recognize when you were starting to get upset or frustrated? What did you do to help calm down?

Red Light/Green Light

Red Light/Green Light is a fun group activity that capitalizes on the use of physical space to help clients develop better attentional and impulse control skills. The activity is a fun way to introduce and practice both the mental and physical task of stopping before performing an action. You will need a space to run & play for this activity.

Directions

1. Designate one client in the group to be the "caller." Have the remaining group members line up on one side of the space, with the caller standing at least 50 feet ahead. The caller should have their back turned away from the rest of the group.

2. When the caller yells, "Green light," clients run as fast as they can toward the caller.

3. When the caller yells, "Red light," each runner has to freeze in their tracks. Anyone who moves is out of the game.

4. The caller continues alternating between yelling, "Green light" and "Red light," until one person reaches the caller during green light and touches their arm.

Reflection and Discussion Questions

1. Was it hard to stop when you heard, "Red light"? Why?

2. Did you find any tricks to helping you stop?

Be a Turtle

Teaching children ways to manage emotions is a tool that will help them in all areas of their life. Yoga and mindful interventions allow students to take a break and pause their mindset while they use coping strategies to self-regulate. This is a hands-on activity that helps children understand the concept of taking a break when they need to use regulation strategies. You will need a space to play for this activity.

Directions

1. Explain that when turtles get scared or sad, they retreat into their shells until they are able to come out again feeling calm and safe.

2. Open a discussion about times when someone might feel sad or scared, and review strategies for managing those feelings (e.g., belly breathing/deep breathing, counting, etc.).

3. Describe how we can all be like a turtle when we feel that way by closing our eyes and imagining that we are retreating into our shell to use our strategies.

4. Model being a turtle by getting down on the ground in a turtle pose (on your knees, with your hands crouched into a ball). Demonstrate sticking your head out of your shell and then retreating in. When you retreat in, close your eyes and take four deep breaths or count to ten slowly.

5. Finish by demonstrating that this strategy calmed you down enough to stick your head out again because you felt safe and calm.

6. After you have modeled being a turtle, ask clients to join in.

7. Practice this at least three times with the group, and then use the following questions to discuss and reflect on the exercise.

Reflection and Discussion Questions

1. How did it feel to be a turtle?

2. What strategy did you use?

3. Can you think of other strategies you might use when you feel upset?

Friendship Pillowcases

Creating friendship pillowcases is a fun group activity that can help children develop positive self-thoughts by getting positive feedback from those around them. By counteracting their negative thoughts with more uplifting ones, clients begin to increase self-esteem and self-confidence, leading to more happiness.

Materials

- White pillowcases
- Fabric markers
- Timer (bell, chime, or music)
- Stencils (optional)

Directions

1. Gather the group into a large circle, and give each client a plain white pillowcase and a variety of fabric markers.

2. Instruct everyone to lay their pillowcases out flat in front of them, making sure to leave enough room between each pillowcase (at least one foot on each side if possible).

3. Ask each client to write their name in the middle of their pillowcase and to draw a decorative border around their name.

4. Explain that this is a friendship pillowcase and that each person is going to be given an opportunity to write at least one thing that they really like about each member of the group. They can also draw pictures if there is time, but they must write at least one thing.

5. When the timer goes off, everyone in the group will move to the pillowcase to their right, and each person will have five minutes for that particular pillowcase. If clients finish early with the writing portion, then they can draw something for that person as well.

6. Once the group has finished, have everyone take a moment to review what others have written about them and share with the group if desired.

7. Explain that every time they feel lonely or are in need of a friend, they can use this pillowcase at night. It will remind them of how special they are to these friends.

Reflection and Discussion Questions

1. How did it feel to read what people wrote about you?

2. Were you surprised by anything written?

Water Bead Stress Ball

Creating a water bead stress ball is a hands-on sensory activity that can help with stress and anxiety—both in terms of making the stress ball, which is an anxiety-reducing activity, as well as having a final product that clients can take with them because it is small and portable.

Materials

- Latex balloons
- Water beads
- Water
- Bowl
- Plastic bottles

Directions

1. Depending on the client's ability and developmental level, they may participate in making the stress ball or just assist in various steps within these directions. Use your discretion based on your knowledge of the client.

2. Place a small handful of water beads in a bowl and fill it with water.

3. Let it sit for at least six hours, and then drain the water from the bowl.

4. Place the remaining full water beads in an empty plastic water bottle, either by hand or with a funnel.

5. Place the balloon opening over the top of the water bottle opening, and squeeze the beads into the balloon.

6. Pull the balloon off, and let the excess air out of the balloon before tying it tightly.

7. Tuck the tied portion inside the balloon.

8. After creating the stress ball, demonstrate how to use it and have clients play around with it.

Reflection and Discussion Questions

1. Did you like the texture of the beads?

2. Do they feel different in the balloon when they are used as a stress ball?

3. When do you think you might use this?

Magic Wand Wishes

Many times, it is difficult for clients to see solutions because they are caught up in the problem. By providing them with a way to see possible solutions, you can open them up to detailing a way to get to those solutions step by step. To do so, this activity incorporates the "miracle question" intervention from BSFT through the use of a magic wand.

Materials

- Small styrofoam ball
- Accessories (e.g., sticky jewels, ribbon, pipe cleaner, etc.)
- Popsicle stick or longer wooden dowel

Directions

1. Have clients create a "magic wand" by decorating a styrofoam ball and then sticking it to the end of the popsicle stick or dowel.

2. Ask clients to talk about a problem they have and to use the magic wand to create a magical solution. For example: "Imagine that you wave this wand and *POOF*! Your problem is solved. What would that look like?"

3. Ask clients to describe what would be different about life in a world where this problem no longer exists.

4. Walk the client through the steps that they might take in their current life to move closer to that new world.

Reflection and Discussion Questions

1. When could you use this wand at home? At school?
2. What steps that you identified do you think you might be able to start with now?

Problem-Solving Origami

When children are in school, it is inevitable that they will experience conflict with their peers at one time or another. This activity helps introduce and reinforce the use of problem-solving strategies to overcome social conflict through the use of origami. In particular, children create an origami fortune teller (also known as a "cootie catcher") containing various problem resolution skills that they can reference in times of social conflict. This fun activity allows clients to create a product to take with them to use outside of the session.

Materials

- Origami instruction sheet
- Problem-solving origami template(s)

Directions

1. Begin by asking clients if they have ever tried origami, and briefly explain how origami involves the art of paper folding.

2. Explain that, sometimes, when we get stuck in a social conflict and don't know what problem-solving strategy to use, it can be fun to use origami to try some different techniques.

3. Go through the instructions for folding and constructing the origami, and then introduce the problem-solving origami template (pgs. 114-115). There is a template with specific problem-resolution skills already included, as well as a blank template where clients can brainstorm other ways to problem solve.

Reflection and Discussion Questions

1. When could you use this origami at home? At school?

2. Do you think you could teach others to use this?

Origami Instructions

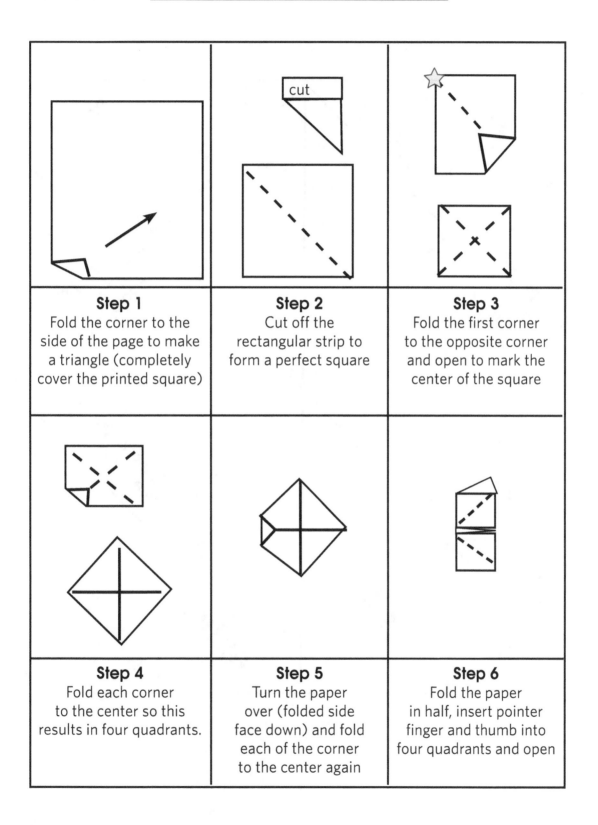

Step 1
Fold the corner to the side of the page to make a triangle (completely cover the printed square)

Step 2
Cut off the rectangular strip to form a perfect square

Step 3
Fold the first corner to the opposite corner and open to mark the center of the square

Step 4
Fold each corner to the center so this results in four quadrants.

Step 5
Turn the paper over (folded side face down) and fold each of the corner to the center again

Step 6
Fold the paper in half, insert pointer finger and thumb into four quadrants and open

Problem-Solving Origami Template

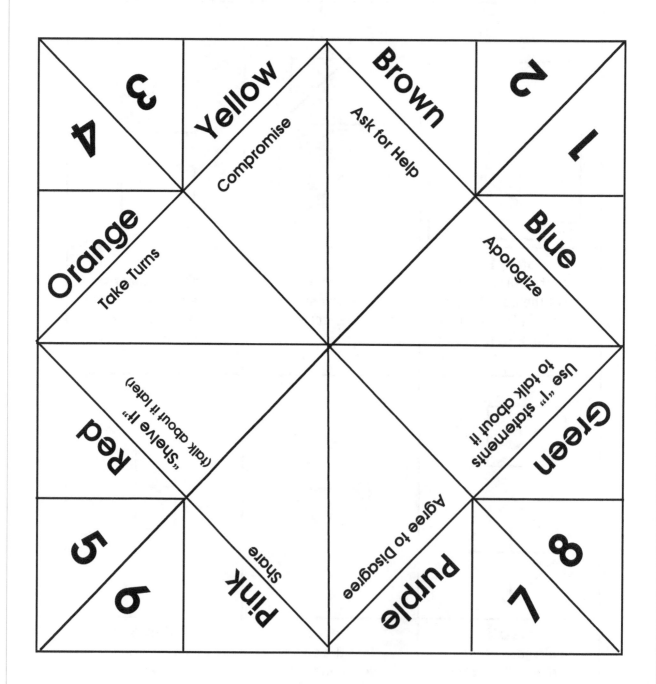

Blank Origami Template

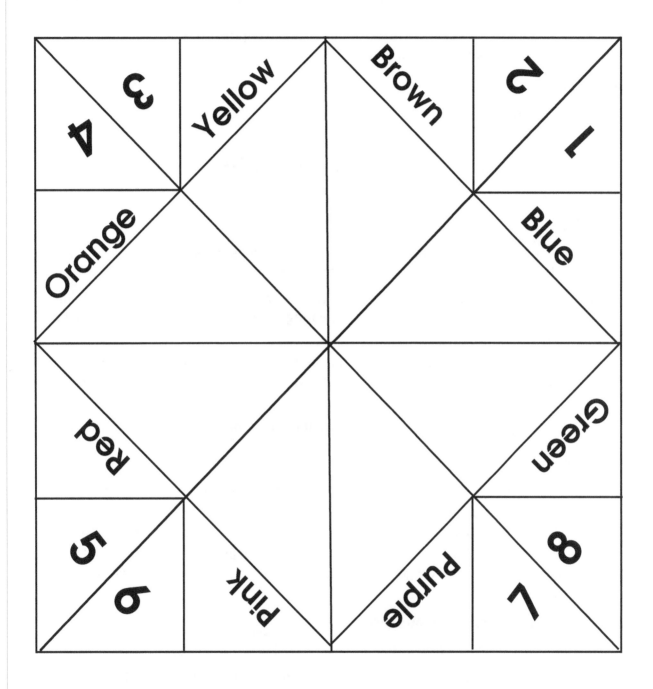

The Control Circle

This activity uses physical space to help children understand the concept of things that are in and out of their control. In particular, it provides a visual for them to see the things they do have control over in order to make those a focus of their time instead of increasing worry about the things they cannot control.

Materials

- Ball of string
- Scissors
- Small pieces of paper, Post-it notes, or 3 x 5 index cards
- Pencils or pens

Directions

1. Explain to clients that you will be talking about things in their life that are *in* their control, as well as things that are *out* of their control.

2. On each piece of paper, ask clients to write down different things about their life that they can and cannot control (e.g., eating, sleeping, homework, going to school, going on a family vacation, etc.).

3. Use the string to create one large circle on the floor. Point out to clients that there is a space inside the circle, as well as outside the circle.

4. Ask clients to place the pieces of paper in the corresponding area of the circle: Everything they wrote down that is *in* their control should go in the center of the circle, and everything that is *out* of their control should be placed outside the circle.

5. For any items that are unclear, take the time to discuss and place them in or out of the circle accordingly.

6. Reflect on the exercise by discussing the importance of putting our time and energy into the situations that we can control. For example, we can't control the amount of homework we get, but we can control the amount of time we spend studying.

Reflection and Discussion Questions

1. Was this easy or uncomfortable for you? Why?

2. Did you see more things in your life that were in or out of your control? Were you surprised by this?

3. How do you think you might be able to use this in the future?

Colored Candy Regulation

This group activity uses different colored candies to help children practice various emotion-regulation strategies. By understanding and expanding regulation strategies in their toolbox, it allows them to more easily access a tool when feeling emotionally escalated.

Materials

- Skittles® or other colored candy
- Opaque bag or box to hold the candy

Directions

1. Join the group members in a circle and review the five different emotion regulation strategies provided on the following page:

   - Belly breathing
   - Lemon squeeze (holding pretend lemons in your hand(s) and squeezing to make lemon juice)
   - Doing jumping jacks or wall push-ups
   - Telling a funny joke
   - Demonstrating a yoga pose

2. Explain that, in this activity, each color candy will represent one of these strategies.

3. Pass the bag or box of candies to the first person in the circle, and ask them to take one candy out and give an example of a time when they needed to use that strategy to calm down.

4. Have the client lead the group by demonstrating that strategy. Let clients know that they are not allowed to eat the candy until they demonstrate the strategy!

Reflection and Discussion Questions

1. Was this easy or uncomfortable for you? Why?
2. What is your favorite strategy to use? Why?
3. What is your least favorite strategy to use? Why?

RED

Show us belly breathing with five deep breaths

GREEN

Show us the lemon squeeze with both hands

YELLOW

Show us five jumping jacks or wall push-ups

PURPLE

Tell us a funny joke

ORANGE

Show us how to do a yoga pose (your choice)

Sphere Breathing

Sphere Breathing is a fun exercise that introduces and encourages the practice of using deep breathing by pairing it with a physical tool that expands and contracts along with clients' stomachs as they breathe in and out.

Materials

- Hoberman sphere

Directions

1. Introduce or review the steps involved in deep breathing:

   "Breath in for a count of four through your nose.
   Hold for a count of four.
   Breath out for a count of four through your mouth."

2. Introduce the Hoberman sphere, and allow the client to play around with opening and closing it.

3. Model how to pair breathing in and out with the sphere:

   "Open the sphere as you breathe in, hold it in place as you pause your breath, and then close it as you breathe out. It should be fully expanded at the end of your in-breath and fully collapsed by the end of your out-breath."

Reflection and Discussion Questions

1. Was this easy or uncomfortable for you? Why?

2. Do you think you can do this without the sphere?

Thinking Putty

Fidgets have become mainstream in helping children with attention challenges focus in settings that require them to sustain focus for a longer period of time. Putty, slime, and other sensory tools have been found to be effective ways of achieving this goal. The following make-and-take activity allows clients to create "thinking putty" that they can use as a fidget whenever they need to.

Materials

- Access to a sink or cleanup materials
- Bowl
- Ziploc® container or other airtight container
- Recipe ingredients:
    - One cup cornstarch
    - Three to four ounces lotion
    - Food coloring (optional)
    - Essential oils (optional)

Directions

1. Discuss what a fidget is and why it is useful in helping some people when they are distracted or need to calm down.

2. Prior to the session, make a batch of thinking putty so you can introduce clients to the final product, letting them feel and stretch it themselves.

3. Give clients the following recipe and let them create their own version. Clients can use different colors and/or scents to personalize their putty.

    - Add one cup of cornstarch to the bowl.
    - Add lotion to the bowl and mix it together with a spoon.
    - Knead the ingredients together as it becomes harder. If it is too sticky, add more cornstarch until the desired consistency is reached.
    - Add one to two drops of essential oils, as desired. You can also add food coloring.
    - Store in an airtight container.

Reflection and Discussion Questions

1. Was this easy or uncomfortable for you? Why?

2. When do you think you might use this thinking putty?

Slo-Mo on the Go

Slowing down and making meaningful movements to express ideas, thoughts, and emotions is a way to help clients start to understand both their emotions and the reactions and actions of others. This exercise helps clients practice engaging in mindful movement through the use of real-life scenarios.

Materials

- 3 x 5 index cards
- Pens or pencils
- Stopwatch

Directions

1. Using two separate cards, ask clients to write down two things that they do inside or outside of school. For example, this can include doing homework, taking a test, playing soccer, shopping, etc.

2. When they are finished, have the client place the cards upside down on a table or in a pile on the floor.

3. Explain that you will choose one card at a time and the client will act out whatever is on the card in slow motion for one minute.

4. Choose a card and start the timer while the client acts out the scenario on the card.

5. If in a group format, repeat until the cards are gone.

Reflection and Discussion Questions

1. Was this easy or uncomfortable for you? Why?

2. Was it hard to move in slow motion? If so, why do you think it was so hard to move slowly?

Up, Up, and Away

Understanding the impact that positive and negative thoughts can have on our emotions and self-esteem is crucial in helping clients make the change in replacing the negative thought loop. Through the use of balloons and weights, this group exercise provides children with a concrete way to think about positive and negative thoughts.

Materials

- Two helium balloons (with string attached) for each client
- Small weights (heavy enough to weigh down a balloon)
- 3 x 5 index cards
- Paper
- Pens or pencils
- Tape

Directions

1. Ask clients to brainstorm a list of both positive and negative thoughts that they have.

2. Once they have finished creating the list, have them choose one positive thought and one negative thought from the list, and instruct them to write these thoughts down on two separate cards.

3. Explain that thoughts influence our feelings and behaviors: Negative thoughts weigh us down, while positive thoughts lift us up and make us feel lighter and happier.

4. Ask clients to tape a small weight to their negative thought card. Then, have clients hold the positive and negative card (including the weight) in each hand. Have clients notice the difference and discuss what it is like for them.

5. Have clients tie or tape each card onto a balloon. Ask clients to hold each balloon out in front of them and let go of both balloons at the same time. Point out how one balloon drops to the floor and becomes immobile, while the other floats and dances around the room.

6. Come back as a group and discuss.

Reflection and Discussion Questions

1. Was this easy or uncomfortable for you? Why?

2. What did you take away from the two balloons experiment?

Mindful Jar

In this make-and-take activity, clients create a mindful or calming jar that they can use whenever they need help to calm their emotions and settle their mind. The activity not only uses a visual metaphor about how they may settle their thoughts and emotions, but it also gives them a visual timer to match their breathing as they watch the glitter settle to the bottom of the jar.

Materials

- Access to a sink or cleanup materials
- A jar or plastic container with a watertight lid
- Hot glue gun
- Decorative accessories (e.g., ribbon, jewels, etc.)
- Recipe ingredients
  - Warm water
  - One to two tablespoons of vegetable glycerin
  - One to two drops of clear dish soap
  - Glitter (various colors)
  - Food coloring (optional)

Directions

1. Discuss what a mindful jar is and demonstrate its use:

   "When you feel overwhelmed and cannot think clearly, you feel just like this jar when it is shaken up. However, when you use some strategies to calm down, your mind becomes clearer—just like this glitter settling in the jar. Whenever you are feeling upset, you can use this mindful jar by shaking it, setting it down, and practicing deep breathing until you see all the glitter settle to the bottom."

2. Give clients the instructions for creating a mindful jar and let them create their own version:
   - Add warm water to the jar or container, filling it three-fourths of the way up.
   - Add as little or as much of glitter or food coloring as you'd like.
   - Add the glycerin and drops of soap to keep the glitter from clumping.
   - Put hot glue on the inside of the lid and twist it closed tightly.
   - Decorate the lid as desired.

Reflection and Discussion Questions

1. How did it feel to do deep breathing while the glitter settled?
2. When do you think you might use this mindful jar?

You're My Rock

We see things every day, but do we *really* see them? This group activity helps children practice the technique of mindful seeing, in which they learn to be fully present in the moment and pay attention to what it is that they see around them.

Materials

- Variety of rocks that differ in size, shape, texture, color, etc. (enough for each client)
- Paints or paint pens
- Paintbrushes

Directions

1. Gather clients into a group and present them with a tray containing a variety of different rocks.

2. Allow them to view the rocks for approximately ten seconds, and then ask the group to list or verbalize what they saw. Were all the rocks the same?

3. Have clients sit in a circle and pass the rocks around, asking each client to take one rock and place it in front of them.

4. Ask each client to describe the rock in front of them in as much detail as possible, including whether it has spots, lines, is more than one color, whether it is rough or smooth, etc.—something unique about it.

5. Explain that when you look at something closely, you often see things that you didn't see before. By paying close attention, things tend to become clearer and more in focus.

6. Direct the group to try to memorize as much as they can about their rock, and then ask them to return it to the tray.

7. Once all the rocks are returned, instruct clients to go to the table and try to find "their rock" by looking at them again with "new eyes."

8. Explain that this rock is now their own personal focus rock that can be used for times of reflection and mediation, or just as a paperweight (whatever they desire).

9. Provide the group with the opportunity to use the paints to personalize their rock to take home.

Reflection and Discussion Questions

1. Was it easier to find the rock after you spent time closely looking at it? Why or why not?

2. When do you think you might use your rock?

Mind Your Senses

Most of us don't use all our senses when encountering daily things. We tend to move through our daily lives without paying attention to the things around us. This mindfulness exercise is meant to assist clients in becoming more mindfully aware of their senses of smell, touch, and taste—as opposed to relying on their sense of sight alone. We tend to use our vision as a primary sense, and taking it out of the equation allows clients to practice using other senses.

Materials

- Edible items (that are not potentially highly allergic) but that also have a strong smell. Examples might include: orange, banana, popcorn, tomato, lemon, or chocolate.
- Blindfolds
- Pens
- Mind Your Senses worksheet

Directions

1. Group clients in pairs or small groups of no more than four.
2. Let them know that they will be asked to wear their blindfolds and use their other senses (e.g., taste, touch, smell) to guess what food item is in front of them.
3. Explain to clients that after they have touched, smelled, and tasted the item, they can remove their blindfolds and take a quiet moment to write down their observations on the Mind Your Senses worksheet provided on the following page.
4. Distribute the food items (same for each group) to each group and allot approximately three to five minutes to finish the activity.
5. Come back as a group and use the following questions to review the exercise.

Reflection and Discussion Questions

1. What was the experience like for you?
2. Did you find one sense more difficult to use and describe than another?
3. Were you surprised at all by any part of the experience?

Mind Your Senses Worksheet

1. What was your first thought when you touched the item?

   _____

2. Describe what you felt in three words:
       1. _____
       2. _____
       3. _____

3. What was your first thought when you smelled it?

   _____

4. Describe the smell in three words:
       1. _____
       2. _____
       3. _____

5. What was your first thought when you tasted it?

   _____

6. Describe the taste in three words:
       1. _____
       2. _____
       3. _____

7. What did you think this item was?

   _____

Engineering Puppeteering

The use of puppets allows clients to not only create an individualized puppet that is true to their experience, but it also unleashes the creativity and imagination related to puppet use in therapy. In this exercise, clients will create a personalized puppet character that they can use to play out a variety of scenarios (either real-life or imagined) and build on their problem-solving and conflict-resolution skills.

Materials

- Socks (preferably knee-high)
- Various accessories (e.g., yarn, thread, buttons, sequins, feathers, etc.)

Directions

1. Use the accessories provided to create a unique individualized puppet by sewing them onto the sock. (The client may participate as much as possible depending on their ability and developmental level.) If more than one sock is available, create a number of characters to use in the session.

2. Use the sock puppets to recreate real-life situations (or possible scenarios) in order to help clients problem solve and develop solutions.

3. Some possible themes to consider include:

   - Social skills
   - Emotion regulation
   - Separation anxiety, test or school-related anxiety

Reflection and Discussion Questions

1. What was your favorite part of this activity?
2. Do you think you will use the puppet at home? If so, how?

Flip the Script Card Game

To change the negative thought processes that interfere with confidence and self-esteem, clients need to substitute positive thoughts in their place. However, this can be challenging for clients who have become habitually focused on seeing life through a negative lens. Turning the process into a game is an easy way to introduce the concept of cognitive reframing and help clients challenge their negative automatic thoughts. When this game is played in the context of a group, the competition can also help motivate clients to participate.

Materials

- Playing cards (Preprinted and blank cards are provided on the following pages.) The cards are easiest to use when printed on cardstock and laminated.

- Pens or pencils

Directions

1. Shuffle the cards and lay them in a pile facedown. Flip the first card up and place it next to the stack.

2. Read the statement or scenario written on the card out loud to the group.

3. The first client to call out, "Flip the script," and change the statement to something positive gets to keep the card.

4. The client with the most cards at the end of the deck wins!

5. Initially, use the preprinted cards to play the game, but as clients disclose more examples of negative automatic thoughts during your discussions, ask them to write these thoughts down on the blank cards to use in future sessions.

Reflection and Discussion Questions

1. Was this easy or difficult for you? Why?

2. Were there any thoughts that were harder to flip the script on than others?

3. Do you think you can flip the script in situations at school and home?

Flip the Script Playing Cards

I suck at math.	I thought Pat was my friend, but she hasn't called me since last week, so I guess she hates me now.	Maybe if the teacher didn't assign us so much homework I could get it done.
Since he isn't talking to me, I guess I said something that was wrong.	The teacher doesn't like me because she never calls on me in class.	At recess people never ask me to play with them.
I only scored one goal, and I am sure that is why my team lost on Saturday.	I am going to fail that test, and then I will never get into college or have a good career.	I always get those math problems wrong. My teacher thinks I am stupid.

I'm not even going to ask for help from my teacher anymore because I raised my hand and he didn't even call on me.	I didn't get invited to Tony's party, so I am sure everyone thinks I am a loser.	I worked so hard to finish my science project, but I didn't win first place, so it must have been the worst.
Tomorrow is the big game, and I know I am going to let everyone down.	I snapped at Jesse today when he asked if I was okay. I am so stupid, and I am sure he thinks I am a jerk.	Oh my gosh! I didn't finish checking my work before I turned it in. I am sure I will totally fail.
I never get a turn in that game.	Ugh! I got 80% on that test. I should have gotten 100%.	I see my friends in a group over there laughing. I know they are laughing at me.

Range of Feelings Bingo

Many young clients have a simple repertoire of feelings. Their feelings vocabulary is limited, and the idea that feelings fall on a continuum or have a range is a new idea. This game helps introduce this concept through the familiar and fun bingo strategy.

Materials

- Bingo boards (provided on following pages)
- Feelings cards (To make the feelings cards, make an extra copy of the bingo card and cut out/laminate the feelings.)
- Bingo markers (e.g., small stickers, pennies, or paper circles)
- Pens or pencils

Directions

1. This bingo game is slightly different than others because the boards are very similar. They all include a spectrum of a specific feeling, which ranges from mild to intense. For example, calm to happy to joyful to ecstatic. Although each board may have differently-placed feelings on them, the spectrum is the same in order to provide consistency.

2. Just like a traditional bingo game, have each client choose a bingo board that they will use for the game. You can choose to either keep the boards unlaminated and have clients write on them, or you can laminate the boards and have clients use a type of marker.

3. Prior to starting the game, review the feelings with the clients, if you have not done so before. Then, shuffle the feelings cards and pull a card out one at a time. When you call out the feeling on each card, have clients find it on their board and cover it.

4. Once a client completes a horizontal line, they shout out, "Bingo," and the name of the feeling (e.g., "Bingo! Happy!").

Reflection and Discussion Questions

1. What did you like about this version of bingo?
2. Was it hard to lose (or win)? Why or why not? How did you handle it?

Bingo Boards

Calm	Happy	Mad	Ecstatic
Agitated	Annoyed	Joyful	Furious
Melancholy	Disappointed	Sad	Depressed

Annoyed	Joyful	Happy	Ecstatic
Melancholy	Disappointed	Depressed	Furious
Agitated	Calm	Mad	Sad

Melancholy	Disappointed	Mad	Depressed
Agitated	Annoyed	Sad	Furious
Calm	Happy	Joyful	Ecstatic

Agitated	Annoyed	Calm	Furious
Mad	Sad	Joyful	Ecstatic
Melancholy	Disappointed	Happy	Depressed

Chapter 7

Drama Directives

Using drama in counseling gives clients a way to express their thoughts and feelings through the use of theatrical tools and techniques. Drama not only provides a fun venue through which clients can practice various ways of interacting with other people, but it also gives them an opportunity to practice or rehearse other strategies and behaviors that they might not have a chance to do regularly outside of the counseling environment. Engaging in role-play and observing others do the same simultaneously promotes the development of interpersonal skills and helps clients increase their self-awareness and positive sense of self.

On the following pages, you will find 19 drama directives that you can integrate into the context of your counseling sessions. Some of the common techniques you will find in these directives include:

- **Scripted role**: Clients study a premade script and use it to act out a scene or character.
- **Improvisation**: Clients act out scenes or characters with minimal information or guidance.
- **Storytelling**: Clients act out or create and tell a story.
- **Projective play**: Clients use objects, props, or toys to express feelings about certain topics or experiences.
- **Miming**: Clients use movement without speech to act out a scene or emotion.

The Director

In this psychoeducational drama, clients practice reflective and listening skills to see a situation through a new perspective. It gives the person acting as director the opportunity to see a situation through the eyes of other group members as they act out scenes that the director has set up.

Materials

- Groups of three

Directions

1. Divide clients into groups of three.

2. Have clients discuss and decide on a conflict scene they would like to act out. Ideally, this conflict situation should represent something that people in the group are currently experiencing.

3. Allow clients to decide who will be the director and who will act out the scene.

4. At the start of the scene, the actors freeze in place, and the director positions their bodies to reflect how they envision the scene beginning. This process includes positioning the actor's facial expressions, hands, body posture, etc.

5. Once the scene is set, the director says, "Action!"

6. The actors start from their positions and act out the scene based on how they are currently positioned, reflecting how the director sees it and not how the actors interpret it. For example, they may decide to reenact a bullying incident that took place for the director. Therefore, the director would position each of the actors in place, and the actors would start acting based on how they have been positioned and the information the director has given them. The point is to mirror the conflict back to the director as clearly as possible, without trying to solve the conflict or address the problem in any way.

Reflection and Discussion Questions

1. Was this an easy or difficult task? How so?

2. If you were the director, did the way the actors responded in acting out your scene surprise you?

3. If you were an actor, was it difficult to act out the scene that someone had set up for you?

Mirror, Mirror

In this exercise, clients pair up with a partner and act as if they are a mirror of that person. By mirroring their partner's movements and facial expressions, clients practice reading social cues, and they also build on emotion regulation and self-awareness skills by understanding how others may see them in a concrete visual format.

Materials

- Timer

Directions

1. Group clients into pairs and have each dyad stand facing each other.

2. Explain that they will choose who will be the "actor" first and who will be the "mirror."

3. The client serving as the actor will have one minute to create movements that the other person will have to "mirror" or copy exactly as if they were a mirror in front of the other person. These movements can include facial expressions, body posture, etc.

4. Once the timer is done, have the clients switch roles.

Reflection and Discussion Questions

1. What was the most difficult part of this task? Why?

2. What was it like mirroring the other person?

The Instrument

This partner exercise is a great icebreaker to help clients familiarize themselves with one another. It is also a way to introduce collaborative problem solving with peers as they each have to work and interact with other clients to become the musician and get the instrument to work. This activity requires an even number of clients to participate.

Materials

- Timer

Directions

1. Explain that clients will be partnering up with someone else to practice taking on the role of an instrument and a musician.

2. Have clients group into pairs and decide who will start as the "instrument" and who will be the "musician."

3. The person playing the role of the instrument decides what sound to make and performs it with one single out-breath. The "instrument" then repeats this same sound for each subsequent breath (amount determined by you as the facilitator) while the musician plays the instrument.

4. To change the instrument's sound, the musician alters the instrument's body in a variety of ways. For example, the musician can move the instrument's arms, tap on their head, or squeeze their fingers. Each different movement serves to change the sound that the instrument makes. Only the musician can alter the sounds (*not* the instrument).

5. Have the dyads continue this process for two minutes and then switch roles.

Reflection and Discussion Questions

1. Was this an easy or difficult task? Why?

2. How did it feel to be the instrument?

3. How did it feel to be the musician?

Adapted from Pendzik (2008)

And Then...

This creative storytelling exercise can be used in an individual or group format to help clients understand different perspectives. When used in a group format, clients practice empathy by acting out the stories that other group members have written.

Materials

- Paper
- Pencil or pen
- Timer

Directions

1. Explain to clients that they will be given a starter sentence and asked to complete the sentence by writing a short story.

    - If this exercise is being done in a group format, explain that everyone's story ending may be different and that these endings will be used in a subsequent activity.

2. Give clients the following prompt: *"It was Casey's first day at her new school. Casey got ready that morning and..."*

3. Set a timer for five minutes and instruct clients to finish the story however they wish. Give them a one-minute warning to allow them enough time to finish up writing.

4. Once the clients have completed their stories, collect their responses and redistribute them among group members. (It is okay if someone gets their own story.)

    - Use the stories to pair up clients in order to act out each of the stories for the group.

    - If there is only one client, work with them to decide how to act it out together.

5. After role-playing the entire story, answer the following questions.

Reflection and Discussion Questions

1. Was this an easy or difficult task? Why?

2. What did it feel like to act out your story?

3. Was there anything in the story that you have felt before? Was it related to any real-life experiences?

Role-Play

Understanding how our reactions vary across situations (both in terms of how we feel and the response we get from others) is an important skill to learn. We may respond either positively or negatively, which then determines how we feel and what we remember about it, as well as our next actions. This activity invites clients to explore the impact of both positive and negative reactions to the same scenario through role-play.

Materials

- Role-play cards
- Timer

Directions

1. In this exercise, clients will be using role-play cards (provided on the next page) to act out a variety of different scenarios with ambiguous endings. Clients will act out what might be the positive or negative ending involved in each scenario. Two blank cards are also provided so you can create your own scenarios for clients to act out as well.

2. Choose a role-play card and read it out loud.
   - If being conducted in a group format, instruct clients to act out the positive or negative ending to the scene.
   - If being conducted in an individual format, act the scene out with the client, following the client's lead.

3. Review the role-play exercise by answering the following questions.

Reflection and Discussion Questions

1. Was this an easy or difficult task? Why?
2. Was it easier to role-play the positive or negative version?
3. What was your favorite card to act out?

Role-Play Cards

You quietly walk into the kitchen to sneak a cookie from the cookie jar…

A teacher turns around in class to find one of your peers passing a note to you…

You come home to find a letter addressed to you. You open it and…

You are shopping with a friend and you see her take something and put it under her sweater…

Puppet Show

When children experience a difficult or traumatic event, they often process it through repetitive play of the event itself. This can take place with small events, such as a fight with a friend that didn't end positively, as well as larger events, such as a family death or parental divorce. Putting on a puppet show is a great directive to use when clients need a chance to "freestyle" or replay an incident that happened. This activity is best used in a group setting.

Materials

- Various puppets (either homemade or store bought)
- A "stage," which can be developed with a table and blanket, a box with a cutout, or a formal puppet theater

Directions

1. Start by asking clients to list three scenarios to act out that may have caused confusion or stress in the past. Have them write out these scenarios on the board or on a paper near you.

2. Ask clients to choose one of the scenarios they developed. Ask them to choose puppets that are appropriate for the scenario they have been given, and allow them to spend five minutes creating a story around it.

3. Once clients have developed their story, have them take turns using the stage to act out their scenario.

Reflection and Discussion Questions

1. Can you think of a different ending to the story you created?
2. What did you like most about creating the story and puppets?
3. Do you think this story is something other kids might have gone through too?

Role the Dice

This group exercise is a great way to help clients develop greater awareness and understanding of the range of emotions. Each person may have a different way to express, explain, or act out an emotion, which gives the other group members an opportunity to see various ranges of the same feeling. The more clients that you have in this group, the more entertaining it can be, and the more variation you have in your responses.

Materials

- Dice
- Timer

Directions

1. Explain to clients that each number on the dice represents a feeling:

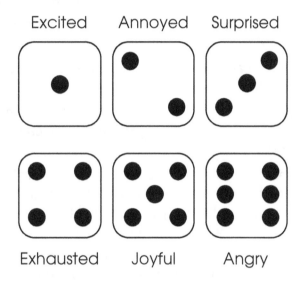

Excited   Annoyed   Surprised

Exhausted   Joyful   Angry

2. Let each player take a turn rolling the dice and acting out the feeling for one minute. Then, ask the other clients to guess the feeling.

Reflection and Discussion Questions

1. How did it feel to do this activity?
2. Was there one feeling that was harder to act out than the others?

Guess My Feeling

This group exercise is a new feelings take on an old party game. It encourages interaction among clients, as well as collaborative problem solving as group members provide each other with clues to figure out the feeling. It also increases understanding of vocabulary around feelings as clients are required to find different ways to explain each feeling word without using the word itself. You will need at least three group members for this activity.

Materials

- Elastic headbands
- 3 x 5 index cards
- Sharpie or felt-tip pen

Directions

1. Ask each client to take two 3 x 5 cards, a headband, and a Sharpie.

2. Instruct clients to write down a different feeling on each card, making sure they write it down big enough to fill the card.

3. Collect and shuffle the cards. Then, pass one card out to each client, placing it facedown in front of them.

4. Ask clients to pick up the card (facing it away from them) and place it under their headband *without looking at it*. For younger clients, you can place the card under their headband for them.

5. Let clients know that their mission is to guess what feeling they have on their headband. To do so, they can walk around the room and ask others to act out what is written on their card in order to try to guess it, but clients must act it out *without using words*.

6. An additional way to play is to allow clients with more developed language skills to use words, but they CANNOT use the actual word on the card. They are allowed to describe things about it and even give scenarios, but the "feelings word" on the card is off limits.

7. Once clients correctly guess their feeling, they can take the headband off and continue acting out for others until everyone has guessed.

Reflection and Discussion Questions

1. How did it feel to have to find ways to help people identify the feeling without using the word to describe it?

2. What was your favorite part of this game?

3. Was it easy for you to guess your word? Why or why not?

Animal Feelings

Sometimes, it helps clients to remove the personalization when talking about a difficult topic. This exercise uses the familiar and nonthreatening form of animals to help clients express feelings and take more risks with dramatic performances. By adopting the form of an animal, it may free them to be more dramatic and share more feelings than if they were required to share as themselves or with a more personal scenario.

Materials

- Animal and feeling cards
- Timer

Directions

1. For this exercise, there are two sets of cards provided on the following pages: one with feelings and one with animals.
2. Give clients a chance to draw one card from each deck and act out the animal with the feeling. For example, if clients draw "cat" and "surprised" out of the deck, then they will practice being a surprised cat during their performance.
3. Ask clients to take turns choosing a card and acting it out for one minute.
4. Continue until everyone has had a turn and/or the deck is completed.

Reflection and Discussion Questions

1. Was this an easy or difficult task? Why?
2. Was it easier to role-play as an animal than it was to play yourself?
3. What was your favorite card combination to act out?

Animal Cards

Elephant	Lion	Dog
Mouse	Cat	Monkey
Squirrel	Bear	Horse

Feelings Cards

Shy	Scared	Excited
Happy	Surprised	Angry
Frustrated	Sad	Nervous

Walking in Their Shoes

This activity helps children develop empathy, and it fosters theory of mind by having them literally and figuratively take a walk in someone else's shoes. Providing clients with scenarios that may be interpreted negatively without understanding the other person's view encourages them to generalize this empathetic viewpoint.

Materials

- Scenario cards (some blank cards are also provided for you to add your own)
- Different pairs of shoes (one set for each client)

Directions

1. Explain to clients that we often don't know what is happening in other people's lives that make them act certain ways. We all have our own shoes that we walk in, and until we are able to put on someone else's shoes and walk in their footsteps, it is hard to understand why they do the things that they do.

2. Provide each client with a pair of shoes, or let clients pick a pair of shoes at random.

3. Let clients know that each set of shoes has a scenario inside and that their job is to read the scenario, step into the shoes, and then act out the scenario.

4. To strengthen clients' ability to understand the perspective of the protagonist in each scenario, use the questions below to facilitate a dialogue about each scenario.

Reflection and Discussion Questions

1. Was this an easy or difficult task? Why?

2. How do you think other people might misinterpret the protagonist's behavior or actions as being "bad" or "different"?

3. Can you think of anyone around you who may be walking in shoes that you don't understand?

Scenario Cards

Casey woke up this morning to a blaring siren outside, and when Casey went downstairs found no milk for cereal so Casey didn't get to eat breakfast.

As Casey walked into school with an empty stomach, in a bad mood, a teacher said, "Hey, Casey just smile - no need to be in such a bad mood today."

What did Casey do next?

Pat was never really confident about math and today there was a big test that was coming in 30 minutes. All of a sudden Pat started to get a really bad stomach ache and racing thoughts of failing the test.

A friend walked over and took Pat's pencil off the desk.

What did Pat do next?

A bully had been targeting Blair on the way home every day but Blair never said anything to anyone out of fear in might get worse.

Blair got to school one day and the teacher had paired Blair with the bully for a school project in class.

What did Blair do next?

Tony's grandfather was really sick last month and this morning Tony's mother left to go be with him because there was a chance he might die soon.

Tony came to school and the teacher told the class there would be a surprise quiz on a history lesson they had last week.

What did Tony do next?

Dani worked hard on a project for the science fair this weekend and was very proud of the results. It was sitting by the front door and Dani's sister accidentally fell on it, breaking a main part. It was due today. Dani came into the class with the project and when the teacher saw it he said, "Dani what have you been doing? Your project isn't finished?"

What did Dani do next?

A crush of Billy's told a friend that they also like Billy. When Billy went up and asked the person he had a crush on to sit him at lunch they just laughed and walked away.

When they went back to class, the teacher asked Billy to get up in front of the class and read a love poem they had been studying.

What did Billy do next?

Pair Up

This partner game teaches clients how to engage in collaborative problem solving in a fun way. Each client may have a different way of problem solving or even a different perspective. By working together, students are encouraged to share their various techniques in order to succeed at the task. This activity requires an even number of clients (at least four, but the more the better!)

Materials

- Music
- Even number of clients (at least four—the more the better!)

Directions

1. Ask clients to roam around the room until they hear you say, "Pair up." Then, each person must find a partner and stand with them.

2. Once everyone is paired with a partner, call out the name of two body parts. Each pair must match these two body parts to each other. For example, one partner must match their nose to the other partner's knee.

3. Partners must stay in this position until another match is called (e.g., hand to foot). However, they must continue to stay in the original position (e.g., nose to knee) while still trying to match this new position as well.

4. Finally, call out, "Release," and play music. Instruct clients to wander around the room until the next round.

Reflection and Discussion Questions

1. Was this an easy or difficult task? Why?
2. What was the hardest part of this game?

What's Happening?

This group activity is a great way to encourage risk-taking (low level with possible embarrassment through performing in front of others) in a safe, supportive environment. It is particularly useful with clients who might not usually feel comfortable stepping out of their comfort zone. For this activity you will need at least four group members.

Directions

1. Have clients gather in a circle, and instruct them to choose one person to start as the performer.

2. The performer then moves into the middle of the circle and starts acting out a nonverbal activity (e.g., making the bed).

3. A different client moves to the circle and asks, "What's happening?" The incoming client then guesses what the performer is doing. If the client is correct, then the performer says, "Yes," and exits the circle.

4. The incoming client then begins performing another task, and the circle continues until all the clients have had a turn.

Reflection and Discussion Questions

1. Was this an easy or difficult task? Why?

2. How did it feel to be in the center of the circle?

It's a . . .

In this activity, clients must think outside the box to come up with a variety of creative uses for a single household item. By visualizing ordinary items in a manner that is beyond their typical use, this activity helps clients develop different perspectives and fosters their imagination. You will need at least three group members for this activity.

Materials

- Various items (e.g., ball, towel, pool noodle, ruler, face mask, paper bag, etc.)

Directions

1. Join clients in a circle and introduce one of the items. Explain that this item can be seen as many different things if we use our imagination. For example, a paper bag can be a hat, a purse, or even a puppet.

2. Pass the object around the circle, asking each client to come up with a different use for, or form of, the object. Allow clients to take a pass if they cannot come up with anything, and return to them in the second round to see if they have an idea.

3. Give the group a goal to think of as many things as they can and to beat their number on the next round or object.

Reflection and Discussion Questions

1. Was this an easy or difficult task? Why?

2. What was your favorite object to use?

The Trickster

When working with children, it can be useful to use drama as a means of identifying and challenging their cognitive distortions. In this activity, clients establish some concrete ways of thinking about distorted thoughts by role-playing an imaginary "trickster" who represents these thoughts. This exercise is best used when clients have previously been introduced to CBT techniques.

Materials

- A hat or other garment used for role-play

Directions

1. Explain to clients that this activity involves role-playing a real-life scenario from the client's experience. This scenario can include a challenging or difficult experience with friends that may have happened at school, or a family event, or a scenario that caused stress or anxiety.

2. Once clients have identified the experience they would like to role-play, have them write it down, including any dialogue.

3. Ask the client to add in any internal dialogue that they had during the experience. This dialogue represents the cognitive distortions that the client had about the experience and will be used as the "trickster's" dialogue during the role-play. For example, if the client is role-playing a situation in which they performed poorly on a test, the internal dialogue about the experience might be, "I am going to fail the class" or "I'm not good at anything."

4. Ask the client to take on one role (either the trickster or themselves) while you take the other. The "trickster" puts on the hat or garment and reads the internal dialogue out loud.

5. Work together with the client to create an opposing rational response. For example, going back to the test, an opposing response might be, "I didn't do well on this test, but I can study hard for the next one."

6. Once you have worked together to create a response, reenact the scene with the rational response, and toss the trickster's hat or garment away.

Reflection and Discussion Questions

1. Was this easy or uncomfortable for you? Why?

2. Why did you choose the role you took on today?

3. How do you think you might be able to use this activity in the future?

Mirror Me

Being able to understand nonverbal cues is a necessary social skill. However, some children may have innate difficulty learning this skill through play and experience, and would benefit from understanding how nonverbal language can communicate what verbal language does not. This partner exercise is a take on charades that encourages clients to read nonverbal cues. You will need an even number of group members.

Materials

- 3 x 5 index cards

Directions

1. Before starting the activity, have a brief discussion with clients about nonverbal language and how we all communicate with both our words and our actions. For example, you may see a friend show another person a new toy they were excited to get, and the friend says, "That's cool," yet rolls their eyes at the same time.

2. Ask each client to write down three feelings on a 3 x 5 card.

3. Collect the cards, and pair each client up with a partner.

4. Shuffle the cards and have both clients in the pair choose one card, making sure that they don't show their card to their partner.

5. Have clients stand face-to-face with their partner, making sure to keep the front of their card hidden from their partner.

6. Have each client in the pair take turns acting out the three feelings written on their card, one by one. Importantly, they must act out the feelings *without using any words*. Once their partner guesses the correct feeling, the client moves on to the next feeling.

7. The first pair to successfully guess all three feelings on each of their cards wins that round.

Reflection and Discussion Questions

1. Was this easy or difficult for you? If so, which part and why?

2. How do you think this might help when you are in a situation and someone is using nonverbal language?

Build a Story

Providing clients with opportunities to work together to problem solve allows them to come up with ideas that they may not have developed on their own. It also helps them learn to understand others' perspectives and see that there is more than "their way" of solving a problem. In this group activity, clients take turns building a story together, which promotes cognitive flexibility and encourages imagination. You will need at least three to four group members for this activity.

Materials

- Timer

Directions

1. Give clients a topic, and tell them that they will be building a story together.

2. Divide the group into one to two actor(s) and two storytellers.

3. Choose one person to start as the first storyteller. The first storyteller gives one sentence to start the story, and the actor acts it out and then freezes.

4. The partner storyteller continues the story by building on to the previous sentence, with the actor again acting out the story and then freezing as they wait for the next storyteller to continue.

5. The storyteller partners continue going back and forth with the story until the timer goes off after three to five minutes.

6. If there is time, mix up the group to allow every person a chance to be a storyteller and actor.

Reflection and Discussion Questions

1. Was this an easy or difficult task? Why?

2. Was it easier to be the storyteller or actor?

3. How was it to share the story development?

Changing Emotions

This exercise uses drama to help clients understand how feelings impact our perception of a situation or even our perception of others in a situation. The activity allows clients to get more than one viewpoint of a situation, which expands their understanding of how other people might react or feel in certain circumstances. You will need at least three group members for this exercise.

Directions

1. Ask the group to come up with a scene from daily life and choose who will act it out. It may include as many people as necessary, with the remaining group members serving as the audience.

2. After they have acted it out neutrally, have the audience choose a feeling and have the actors act out the same scene with that emotion. For example, if two of the four members of the group are acting out a scene about taking a test at school, then the remaining two members could call out, "Excited," when they are done with the original scene. Then, the members would use that feeling to show how the same test-taking situation would look with the feeling of excitement.

3. Repeat the same scene with at least three different emotions before switching actors and repeating the process.

Reflection and Discussion Questions

1. Was this an easy or difficult task? Why?

2. Did you find one emotion more difficult than the others to use in the scenes?

3. What was your favorite scenario?

And the Award Goes to...

It is difficult for many young people to see the positive aspects of themselves. They spend so much time comparing and critiquing themselves that they often forget that others see many positive things about them as well. This group activity helps clients focus on the positive aspects of themselves and others by looking through the eyes of their peers.

Materials

- 3 x 5 index cards
- Pens, crayons, or pencils
- Timer

Directions

1. Give each client a card, and ask them to write their name on one side.

2. Explain that everyone is going to be given an opportunity to write down at least one positive thing about each member of the group.

3. When the timer goes off, everyone in the group will pass their index card to the person sitting to their right, and each person will have five minutes to write down all the positives things they can about the person on the index card.

4. Clients continue passing the index cards around until everyone has had an opportunity to write something positive about each group member.

5. Collect and shuffle the cards. Then, hand out one card to each client, making sure that no one gets their own card.

6. Ask each person to look at their card and think about how they can take all the information on the card to create an award for that person.

7. Explain that they will be presenting the award to that person in a few minutes. They may write notes to be able to use for the presentation.

8. Allow each person to present their award in a ceremonial style to each client.

Reflection and Discussion Questions

1. Was this an easy or difficult task? Why?

2. What did it feel like to receive the award?

3. What did it feel like to give the award?

Alphabet Drama

This activity is a great rapport-building and introductory activity, as it is nonthreatening and uses a familiar topic of the alphabet to introduce the dramatic principle. Integrating drama and the alphabet is a fun and easy way to help foster imagination as well. At least three group members are needed for this exercise.

Directions

1. Explain that the group will work its way through the alphabet by using drama to act out a word for each letter.

2. Identify who would like to go first, and ask that person to start with the first letter of the alphabet. For example, if the client chooses the word "apple" for the letter *A*, then they might act out eating an apple.

3. Once someone guesses the word correctly, clients switch places and move to the next letter.

4. This process continues until the group finishes with the letter *Z*.

Reflection and Discussion Questions

1. Was this easy or difficult for you? If so, which part and why?

2. Did you feel supported by your peers in the group? Why or why not?

References

For your convenience, purchasers can download and
print worksheets and handouts from www.pesi.com/expressive

Arrington, D. (1992). Art therapy with a public school child. In F. E. Anderson, *Art for all the children: Approaches to art therapy for children with disabilities* (2nd ed., pp. 232–270). Springfield, IL: Charles C. Thomas Publisher.

Axline, V. (1947). *Play therapy.* Cambridge, MA: Riverside.

Barnes-Smith, D., Frotz, J., Ito, H., Kohorst, J., & Vascimini, E. (2015). *Expressive arts as a mean of increasing well-being in children* (Thesis). University of Montana, Missoula, MT.

Bergland, C. (2012, December 29). The neuroscience of music, mindset, and motivation. *Psychology Today.* Retrieved from http://www.psychologytoday.com/blog/the-athletes-way/201212/the-neuroscience-music-mindset-and-motivation

Bush, J. (1997). *The handbook of school art therapy: Introducing art therapy into a school system.* Springfield, IL: Charles C. Thomas Publisher.

Centers for Disease Control. (2018). Health care, family, and community factors associated with mental, behavioral, and developmental disorders and poverty among children aged 2–8 years—United States, 2016. *Morbidity and Mortality Weekly Report, 67*(50), 1377–1383.

Clauss-Ehlers, C. (2008). Creative arts counseling in schools: Toward a more comprehensive approach. In H. L. K. Coleman & C. Yeh (Eds.), *Handbook of school counseling* (pp. 517–530). New York, NY: Taylor & Francis Group.

Cochran, J. L. (1996). Using play and art therapy to help culturally diverse students overcome barriers to school success. *School Counselor, 43*(4), 287–298.

DeLue, C. (1999). Physiological effects of creating mandalas. In C. Malchiodi (Ed.), *Medical art therapy with children* (pp. 33–49). Philadelphia, PA: Jessica Kingsley Publishers.

Drachnik, C. (1995). *Interpreting metaphors in children's drawings: A manual.* Burlingame, CA: Abbeygate Press.

Evans, K., & Dubowski, J. (2001). *Art therapy with children on the autistic spectrum: Beyond words.* London, England: Jessica Kingsley Publishers.

Ghandour, R., Sherman, L., Vladutiu, C., Ali, M., Lynch, S., Bitsko, R., & Blumberg, S. (2019). Prevalence and treatment of depression, anxiety, and conduct problems in U.S. children. *The Journal of Pediatrics, 206,* 256–267.

Godfrey, E., & Haythorne, D. (2013). Benefits of drama therapy for autism spectrum disorder: A qualitative analysis of feedback from parents and teachers of clients attending Roundabout drama therapy sessions in schools. *Drama therapy, 35,* 20–28.

Gonzalez-Dolginko, E. (2008). *The secret lives of art therapists: An exploratory study about the nature of the work that art therapists do in schools* (Doctoral dissertation). Hofstra University, New York, NY.

Isis, P. D., Bush, J., Siegel, C. A., & Ventura, Y. (2010). Empowering students through creativity: Art therapy in Miami-Dade County public schools. *Art Therapy: Journal of the American Art Therapy Association, 27*(2), 56–61.

Jones, C., Hart, S., Jimeson, S., Dowdy, E., Earhart, J., Renshaw, T., Eklund, K., & Anderson, D. (2009). Solution-focused brief counseling: Guidelines, considerations, and implications for school psychologists. *The California School Psychologist, 14,* 111–122.

Kazdin, A., & Weisz, J. (2003). *Evidence-based psychotherapies for children and adolescents.* New York, NY: Guilford Press.

Kellogg, J., MacRae, M., Bonny, H. L., & DiLeo, F. (1977). The use of the mandala in psychological evaluation and treatment. *American Journal of Art Therapy, 16*(4), 123–124.

Kuypers, L. (2011). *The zones of regulation.* San Jose, CA: Social Thinking Publishing.

Levitin, D. J. (2006). *This is your brain on music: The science of a human obsession.* New York, NY: Dutton.

Malchiodi, C. A. (Ed.). (2003). *Handbook of art therapy.* New York, NY: Guilford Press.

Malchiodi, C. A. (Ed.). (2005). *Expressive therapies.* New York, NY: Guilford Press.

Malchiodi, C. A. (Ed.). (2008). *Creative interventions with traumatized children.* New York, NY: Guilford Press.

McIntyre, J. (2007). Creating order out of chaos: Music therapy with adolescent boys diagnosed with a behavior disorder and/or emotional disorder. *Music Therapy Today, 8*(1), 56–79.

McKenna, L. (2016, June 1). Boosting social skills in autistic kids with drama. *The Atlantic.* Retrieved from https://www.theatlantic.com/education/archive/2016/06/boosting-social-skills-in-autistic-kids-with-drama/485027/

Murphy, J. J. (2008). Best practices in conducting brief counseling with students. In A. Thomas & J. Grimes (Eds.), *Best practices in school psychology V* (Vol. 4, pp. 1439–1456). Bethesda, MD: National Association of School Psychologists.

Oon, P. (2010). Playing with Gladys: A case study in integrating drama therapy with behavioral interventions for the treatment of selective mutism. *Clinical Child Psychology Psychiatry, 15*(2), 215–230.

Pendzik, S. (2018). Drama therapy exercises. *The Drama Therapy Center.* Retrieved from http://dramatherapycentre.org/exercises/

Phelps, L. (2006). *Chronic health-related disorders in children: Collaborative medical and psychoeducational interventions.* Washington DC: American Psychological Association.

Roland, C. (2006). *Young in art: A developmental look at child art.* Retrieved from http://www.artjunction.org/young_in_art.pdf

Safran, D. S. (2002). *Art therapy and AD/HD: Diagnostic and therapeutic approaches.* London, England: Jessica Kingsley Publishers.

Sausser, S., & Waller, R. J. (2006). A model for music therapy with students with emotional and behavioral disorders. *The Arts in Psychotherapy, 33*(1), 1–10.

Schlechty, P. C. (1990). *Schools for the 21st century.* San Francisco, CA: Jossey-Bass.

Sklare, G. B. (2005). *Brief counseling that works: A solution-focused approach for school counselors and administrators* (2nd ed.). Thousand Oaks, CA: SAGE Publications.

Stepney, S. A. (2010). *Art therapy with students at risk* (2nd ed.). Springfield, IL: Charles C. Thomas Publisher.

Straus, M. (1999). *No-talk therapy.* New York, NY: W. W. Norton.

Urtz, F. P., & Kahn, K. B. (1982). Using drama as an outreach and consultation tool. *The Personnel and Guidance Journal, 60*(5), 326–328.

West, L. (2012). *Art therapy with the developmentally disabled* (Master's thesis). University of Wisconsin, Superior, WI.

Wilson, D. B., Gottfredson, D. C., & Najaka, S. S. (2001). School-based prevention of problem behaviors: A meta-analysis. *Journal of Quantitative Criminology, 17*(3), 247–272.

Wilson, S. J., Lipsey, M. W., & Derzon, J. H. (2003). The effects of school-based intervention programs on aggressive behavior: A meta-analysis. *Journal of Consulting & Clinical Psychology, 71*, 136–149.

Zatorre, R. (2013, June 7). Why music makes our brain sing. *New York Times.* Retrieved from http://www.nytimes.com/2013/06/09/opinion/sunday/why-music-makes-our-brain-sing.html

Zins, J., Weissberg, R., Wang, M., & Walberg, H. (Eds.). (2003). *Building school success on social and emotional learning.* New York, NY: Teachers College Press.